Copyright © 2017 by Lynn Barnes

All rights reserved. No part of this publication may be reproduced, stored in or introduced into a retrieval system, or transmitted, in any form or by any means (electronic, mechanical, photocopying, recording or otherwise), except for brief quotations in printed reviews, without the prior written permission of the publisher or written permission of the publisher of this book.

Library of Congress Control Number: 2017958748
ISBN 978-1979960731
Printed in the United States of America

Dedication

To my family

This book is dedicated to God, the one who brought me through it all. I can't imagine my life without you. You gave me the strength, courage and wisdom to see a way out. No one and nothing can compare to you. To my mom Ernestine Edwards, thank you for showing me how to be strong in the midst of complete chaos. You are my hero not the other way around. I love you. To my dad Leonard Edwards, thank you for being the man you are. I thank you for our relationship and giving me the tools I needed to be the mother that I am today. If it wasn't for the both of you I would not be here. To my brother Antwan Boyd, thank you for loving me to life. There are no words to express how much you being born saved me. You may say that I saved you, but it is truly the other way around. I look up to you and love you with all my heart and soul. To my sister Brandy Joy Edwards, my ride or die chick. I love you so much you don't even know. We are partners in crime literally. Thank you for always being there for me.

To my Cousin James Strickland, thank you for being the most wonderful cousin in the world. Thank you for being you (Power to our people). To my husband, Kennedy Keon Barnes, for loving me unconditionally, thank you for sticking it out with me. Thank you for being my strength when I was truly weak and thank you being the man God created especially for me. Thank you to my children Chrishea McKinney, Kennedy Barnes Jr. and Kelyn McKinney Barnes for inspiring me to tell my story. Kennedy Barnes Jr. Thank you for making me laugh and helping me see myself in you. You are my sunshine. Kelyn McKinney Barnes I can't picture a day without you. You are truly an amazing child. Thank you for your smile, your singing and your laughter. Thank you to my sister's Perri' and Gladys and my brother David for making me stronger in so many ways. To Pastor Bell and Desma Bell, thank you for being my mentors and helping me grow as a woman, mother, wife and a child of God. Thank you for not letting me go. To my best friend in the whole wide world Gina Day. We may not talk everyday but we can always pick up where we left off. I love you more than words can say. To my sister-cousin Gladys Strickland, thank you for helping me feel beautiful when I didn't. Thank you to my aunts Valeria, Vickie, Nanette, Kim, Melinda and Ella, and my uncles Michael, Harold, Howard, Ronald, Johnny, Kenneth, Larry and Stanley for being in my life and adding significance in ways you will never imagine. To all of my Doc (Divine Order Church) and Destiny family, thank you for encouraging me and pouring into me and my family. Last but not least, Thank you to Clyde Anderson for believing in me and working with me to make this book amazing.

Some names and identifying details have been changed to protect the privacy of individuals.

Table of Content

Introduction
iv

Chapter One:
Being Me
1

Chapter Two:
Daddy's Gone
17

Chapter Three:
My Devil
35

Chapter Four:
Broken
55

Chapter Five:
I Was Lost
73

Chapter Six:
Alone & Unwanted
91

Chapter Seven:
This Can't Be Life
107

Chapter Eight:
On High Alert
127

Chapter Nine:
Little Mother
145

Chapter Ten:
Feeling Like A Freed Slave
165

Chapter Eleven:
Pregnant & Afraid
191

Chapter Twelve:
An Unwanted Trend
209

Chapter Thirteen:
Up the Block & Around the Corner
239

Chapter Fourteen:
Graduation
255

Chapter Fifteen:
Celebrate Recovery
278

Introduction

As I sat and wrote my story for the world to read, I was frightened. The thought of being transparent and naked scared me, but I remember wishing I had something to help me get through it. I needed a guide to show me what I didn't know, reinforce what I did and ultimately help me to see me for who I was created to be.

Through years of abuse and neglect, I lost my innocence which also stole my joy and I had no idea how to reclaim it. I wanted to smile again and just be my mother's daughter, but addiction and abuse forced me to grow up quickly. I had to suck it up, be responsible and act like everything was ok. Although there were times I didn't like myself, I didn't like what I saw in the mirror and I began to believe what my peers said about me was true. I was consumed with loneliness, self-doubt, anger, resentment, bitterness, and addiction.

Hell was real and I was living in it. I was going through life on a surfboard riding the flames. I could feel the fire scorching my skin and the pain was my flesh cooking at unbearable temperatures. Little did I know I was being refined.

I've come to realize that I'm not alone. I wasn't the only one that was and still may be fighting the demons that make us feel like we have no value. I do have fond memories of my life, but much of the bad that has haunted me overshadowed the good and made me feel like I was less than… less than others, less than whole and that my life had no value.

When I began to write down my thoughts, the experience was so therapeutic for me. My goal was to be completely honest and naked as possible to help you know yourself by showing you how I got to know myself. In order to feel valuable and to show others my value, I first had to love myself. See, for so long I've allowed other people to validate me by dictating my worth and I didn't know how to love me. I gave myself away at a discount for so long because I was looking for someone else to love me.

I have struggled with many issues for the majority of my life. I couldn't figure out how to overcome my pain to walk in my purpose. I knew I still had issues I needed to overcome because of the way I jumped when my mother playfully pulled at my pants when we were around my uncle. It was obvious the wounds of molestation were still open and they stung. You can overcome the pain by exploring your past as well as where you are right now to find purpose in your pain. Although at times it was hard for me to understand, I came to realize that everything happens for a reason.

I wasn't the first nor would I be the last to have struggles and neither are you. But I believe what I've learned from my struggles will help others that may have faced or are facing similar challenges and obstacles.

By shining light on my journey, hopefully you will be able to see a path to overcome the obstacles that threaten to derail you or even take your life. When I realized that I loved me, I also saw the errors of some of my reckless ways and that many of the things I went through were meant to strengthen me rather than destroy me.

I overcame my obstacles through faith, being introduced to Jesus Christ and committing to building a relationship with Him. The freedom has blessed me. I have come to the realization that I matter. I now know that God is real and was always with me, He has never left me nor forsaken me. Even during my lowest points when I felt lost and alone, I wasn't.

I pray that my words will help you find the strength to tell your story and allow it to be the therapy you need to see yourself and your own value. The truth is you don't have to remain a prisoner to your past. You can break the chains. But to do that you have to believe in yourself, God and His word.

I found God in the midst of the storm. It didn't happen overnight, instead; it took God strategically putting people in my path for my good, but also those that weren't good for me forced me to seek him. That's how He works. My intention is not to hit you over the head with scripture and preach the importance of being a Christian, but rather to help you understand that there is a way to overcome. I want you to see that no matter what you've encountered you are still fearfully and beautifully made by God. You have a bright future even though your view may be cloudy, making it impossible to see.

I was the daughter of a drug-addicted mother and a father who was absent, due to being in the military. My parents grew up in the St. Louis projects where they met as children. They were strong willed and butted heads often during their on and off relationship that produced three children, my brother Antwan who is eleven months older than I and my sister Brandy who at times called me momma.

I love my father. He was my world and I thought the moon and stars revolved around him. I just wanted to love him and be loved by him, but back then I'm not sure he knew how to do that the way I wanted and needed him to. See, a father is the first of everything to a little girl. He's the first boyfriend, first bodyguard and first gentleman. We look up to them and look to them for standard and rules for boys and men.

I can remember when life was good, but soon those good days became few and far between as I looked for security. Allow this book to serve as your guide to recognize who you are, the opportunity in your obstacles and recognize that you are valuable beyond measure.

I found me and now I have a responsibility to help you find you, and realize that you were created for a purpose. I want to help young girls see who they were created to be and love who they are.

I feel so blessed right now because I realize that I matter. Follow my journey to discover how to find your worth or help someone you care about know theirs.

Beyond What You See

Self-worth

/self ˈwərTH/
The sense of one's own value or worth as a person;
self-esteem; self-respect.

"You have been criticizing yourself for years, and it hasn't worked. Try approving of yourself and see what happens."

~ Louise L. Hay– Eleanor Roosevelt

Lynn Barnes

Chapter One
Being Me

"We ask ourselves, 'Who am I to be brilliant, gorgeous, talented, fabulous?' Actually, who are you not to be?"
— Marianne Johnson

We finally landed at the St. Louis Lambert Airport after a long three-hour flight. Moving back and forth to my grandma's house in St. Louis from California became a normal thing for us. As we walked down the corridor still half asleep and rubbing the crust out of our eyes, I saw a familiar face.

"Uncle Melvin!" I screamed.

"Hey Lynnie, hey Twanie." These were the names given to us by my mom.

"Hi Uncle Melvin," Antwan said with a gazing one eye open.

"Hey!" mom said.

"Hey," Uncle Melvin responded.

"How was the flight?"

"It was okay. I wish we had money to get something to eat," mom said.

"Well, you're the one who left in the middle of the night, so I don't know what to tell you," Uncle Melvin responded.

We gathered our rushed half packed pillow cases and loaded them in my Uncle's brown and tan checker station wagon.

"Put on your seat belts," mom said.

As we drove, I couldn't help but get sad. It set in we were leaving the good life in Long Beach California. I left my school and my best friend Lisa, I didn't even say goodbye. I still think of her to this day. We pulled up to my grandma's overcrowded two story brick house on O'bear Street where there were always people. I can say I loved being at my grandma's house. My grandma was a nurse for years and I can remember her waking up at the crack of dawn to get ready. She would put on the white nurses' dress, white stockings, white shoes and the white hat that resembled a boat, just like in the old movies.

Another familiar memory is sneaking into the goldmine. That's what we use to call my grandma's locked closet where you would find one of those big plastic water bottles filled with nickels, dimes, quarters and my favorite Susan B. Anthony coins. She also had cookies, chips and candy. Grandma even had fur coats, new shoes and clothes in there too. It was a real goldmine. I always felt loved and protected by everyone that entered my grandma's house. It was a safe space, and I felt safe being there. The key word is felt. Soon that feeling of being safe became a vague memory. Grandma's house was a two-story brick home with only two bedrooms. A sun room was added upstairs along with an extra room in the downstairs basement. So, we made it work. My aunt and my two cousins slept in the sun room next to my Uncle Carl and Uncle Shawn's room.

Across the hall was my grams and grandpa's room. My mom slept in the basement when she was there. I think she was using drugs by this time, but she hadn't brought it around my brother and I yet. Our first night at grandma's Twan and I slept in the room with my Uncle Carl and Uncle Shawn.

"Come on baby, put on your night gown," my mom said.

"Okay mommy."

"Antwan, get up here and get ready for bed!" mom screamed down to Twan.

My brother loved being downstairs in the basement or in the kitchen. Mom kissed our foreheads and left out of the room. Later in the evening, my Uncle Shawn followed by my Uncle Carl came in to get ready for bed. I was turned towards the wall so I didn't see them get in the bed. Then the lights went off.

I felt like I had been asleep for only a moment when I heard my Uncle Shawn call my name.

"Lynnie," Uncle Shawn whispered, "Lynnie, come over here."

I remember not hesitating because that was my Uncle and when your family tells you to do something you do it. So, I got out of the bed and looked over to my brother who was knocked out. I continued over to the bed where my two uncles laid and stood by my Uncle Shawn on the outer side of the bed.

"Yes," I said.

"Lay down with me," he said.

So, I did. It was early that morning when my innocence was taken away from me. After it was over, he politely told me to go back to my bed and go to sleep. I don't remember my thoughts after that. I don't even remember falling asleep.

No More Safe Place

I was only five when my safe place became a haunted house. Grandma's house was now scary and dark, a place where the boogie man lived.

We soon moved back to California to be with my dad. My parents had a roller coaster romance that made Twan and I unsure if we were coming or going.

Time had passed in California. One day when my mom, brother and I were sitting in the kitchen eating, and my mom received a devastating phone call.

"Oh, my God no!" mom said as she fell to the wall.

I asked her what was wrong.

"Your grandpa Tom passed away," she said.

My heart sank into my chest. *Not my grandpa!* I thought. He can't be dead. I cried uncontrollably. Grandpa Tom was my grandmother's husband, not my mother's father, but he was the only grandpa I knew. I loved him so much. He sort of reminded me of Dr. Martin Luther King but lighter. He had a distinct mole on the top of his right eyebrow. I don't remember him saying much or ever getting mad.

"Baby it's OK."

I couldn't stop crying, but I wasn't crying over my grandpa's death. A fear came over me and all the darkness flooded back.

"I don't want to go back there."

"Why not?" mom said in confusion.

Hesitantly I responded, "I'm scared to say."

"Wait, what?"

"Afraid to say what?"

My brother was sitting there waiting on the storm with the hail and high winds that usually accompanied my mother's rage to trample through our apartment. Still resistant, my mom gave me this look like, you better tell me or I'm going to whoop you. I knew she wasn't bluffing.

I slowly opened my mouth and spoke the words, "uncle Shawn did something to me." My heart was racing as if I was running a marathon with myself.

"What! When!"

The look on my mom's face was unforgettable. Her anger was evident. The flames that I saw in her eyes scared me. I just knew I was going to get it, but my mom came over and hugged me so hard. She rocked me back and forth as we both cried. My brother on the other hand was upset that he didn't protect me. My mom granted my wish and let my brother and I stay with my dad while she went to St. Louis. I didn't want my mom to bring it up when she got there. I mean, I just lost my grandpa, my grandma just lost her husband and now this. My heart broke for my grandma. I wanted to be buried with my grandpa along with the feelings I had hidden in the deepest part of my body. But I'm glad I didn't have to face my grandma or the boogie man.

Two weeks had passed since my mom left for my grandpa's funeral. I couldn't wait to see her. I guess I just wanted to know if she talked to my uncle Shawn, cursed him out, or if she told my grandma. It felt like I was having a panic attack the closer the time came for her to walk through the door. After hours of waiting, I heard the jingling of keys at the door.

"Mommy!" I bellowed.

"Hey baby."

"How was it?" I asked nervously, "It was sad, and a lot of people were there."

What I really wanted to know was, did she talk to my grandma, but mom didn't say anything else. She just walked to the bedroom to put her bags away.

Should I ask her? I thought to myself.

"Nope, if she doesn't bring it up, I'm not going to."

The Effect of Being Me

I had buried that entire night with Uncle Shawn away, never to come back again. The thought of telling my mom, frightened me even more. When I finally told my mother that Uncle Shawn had molested me, my heart was heavy. With my mother there, I felt that everything would be ok. I felt a sense of security. She was there for me and told me that it wasn't my fault. I had a feeling of peace and security for that moment.

Family was a big part of my life, so this made me feel conflicted. *Is this what family does to you?* I thought. I was taught to trust them because they were the ones that would look out for me, but family violated me and I was bruised because of it. When my mom came back with no news, I lost what was left of my sense of security. I had already lost most of it after being violated by my uncle. Even though Uncle Shawn was a special needs adult, that didn't excuse him for what he did. Now I didn't know what to expect going forward. What if it continued? I had no closure. I was too young to fully understand the dynamics of what was going on. I had no security, and I was alone. The place that was once safe was now gone. My body shut down, and I didn't want to be there. I blocked events and time periods in my memory to cope with the pain. It wasn't until a trigger brought it all back almost a year later.

Letter to My Younger Self

Lynnie,

It wasn't your fault! That didn't happen to you because you were a bad person. You trusted an elder in your family and he abused that trust. This doesn't mean everyone will do the same. At five years old, no little girl should go through that. You will learn to forgive one day and understand that people do things that do not make sense.

Love hurts, but you need to know the difference between getting hurt and letting it hurt you over and over. Don't accept the term victim. Recognize what happened and use it as your strength to empower you to get through the times that seem impossible. Create with love, engage with love, build with love—whatever you do, put your heart into it. Know that each day counts.

Finally, the most important thing to remember is that you are worth it, you can go another day, and you can be happy. Life will not throw you anything you cannot handle or overcome.

Once you start to accept and love yourself and your desired path, the smoke will clear and you will breathe easy again. Be kind to yourself and life will be much brighter.

Sincerely,
Lynn
Your Future Self

Being Me Commentary

Ephesians 4:32 ESV, Be kind to one another, tenderhearted, forgive one another, as God in Christ forgave you.

No one should ever have to experience this hurt. Any abuse is wrong and inexcusable. If you or someone you know has gone through or is going through abuse, molestation or any kind of violation, TELL! Let someone know right away. We want to bury things that have happened to us, but it's not healthy. Parents: know who's around your child. Look for any changes in behavior. Let them know you have their back no matter what. They need to feel that security within you. If you don't, it will lead them down the wrong path of trying to find it in someone or something else.

"You are beautiful I know because I made you."

— God

Reflections For Your Journey

+ Know you are beautiful.

+ Keep an open and honest relationship with your parents.

+ Make a list of sayings or quotes that make you feel encouraged or inspired and keep it where you can see it each day.

+ If you are going through any abuse, TELL!

+ Remind yourself that you are not what happens to you.

+ Don't say hurtful things to yourself.

+ Find someone you can confide in.

Beyond What You See

Journal

Lynn Barnes

Chapter Two
Daddy's Gone

"My dad broke my heart before any boy had a chance to...
I was robbed"
~Lynn Barnes

I remember laying on my daddy, listening to him speak through his chest. I could feel the bass in his voice vibrate through my body. That made me feel safe, like nothing could ever happen to me. He called me baby girl, and I loved it. It's true that a girl's first true love is her father, but without that love the question becomes where does she find it and is it possible to replace it?

I was now nine years old and for three years, my mother, Twan, and I had moved back and forth from St. Louis to California several times. Our lives became an endless cycle that included finding my dad, living with my dad, leaving my dad and then losing contact with my dad, only to find him again.

My dad was in the military and he would leave often for long periods of time, so popping in and out of the picture was normal. When we were with my dad, it was nice. We had picnics in the park, birthday parties and pony rides, but soon all that would change.

I remember my mom and I walking from my grandmother's house down Grand Boulevard. It seemed like we walked for hours. My mom was about five or six months pregnant, but her strides while walking down Grand told a different story. We made it to an apartment complex with glass sidings on the doors. We walked up to the door.

Bang! Bang! Bang! My mom almost hurt her fist on the glass as she knocked on the door. I remember thinking, someone must owe her money. Then I saw someone look out of the glass panels of the door, it was my dad.

"Open up this motherf****** door right now, or I will break it down!" my mother screamed.

I didn't understand what was going on. Why was my dad here? Whose place was this, and why isn't he opening the door for us? The door opened, but I don't remember what happened next. What I do remember is the police showing up and me crying. Apparently, my dad was with another woman.

"Why are you in here with this woman?" mom cried.

But my father had no words for her. This marked a moment in my life where I asked questions about the past. Why couldn't I remember a lot of moments with my dad and what was going on in their relationship? I knew they argued a lot, but assumed it was loving dysfunction. It was good, bad and all the above. I was told that it was a lot of abuse and cheating, but I don't know to what extent.

Shortly after that incident we moved into that apartment with my dad and it appeared my mom had won the battle, but now the question was would she win the war. I was thrilled to be with my dad. Twan and I started school and made friends. We had a lot of family around who all stayed in the same complex. Those were good times.

Good times

I remember being on the floor with my night gown on doing a puzzle, my brother in his pj's playing with his Star Wars action figures while mom watched television. My dad walked through the door.

"Hey, ya'll get dressed," my dad said.

We all looked at my dad with confused expressions on our faces.

"Len it's late." my mom said.

"I know, just get dressed. If we leave now we can make it."

"Make what daddy?" I asked.

"I'm taking ya'll to see Escape from New York."

"Yay!"

It was 1981 and I'll never forget that night. Who knew one of the fondest memories I had of spending time with my dad would be courtesy of a one-eyed mercenary named Snake Plissken, the star of the movie.

We needed more space, so we moved into a town home in Laclede Town a mixed-income federally funded housing project in St. Louis. It was all brick, three stories high and not too far from where we lived before, so we had the same friends and went to the same school. I remember Twan and I going up to the third floor where our rooms where.

"This is my room!" my brother said.

"Well, this is my room," I responded.

I loved my room. I spent most of my time in the closet, playing school with my teddy bears and dolls. My sister Brandy was born shortly after. The ups and downs I experienced made me feel like I was riding a roller coaster while staying in Laclede Town. On one hand, I had my mom and dad together. I had friends to race with, climb trees and play tag with. I had family to go chill with and most of all we were settled. My mom and dad still had their issues but we made it work.

No Reason to Live

I remember my mom going away and I didn't understand why. Where was she? I loved my mom and didn't want to be without her. So, one night I took some of my brother's asthma medication because I wanted to die. If I couldn't be with her, I didn't want to live. I ran to the bathroom as the medicine forced its way back up.

As I laid on the bathroom floor tired from vomiting, my dad walked in.

"What's wrong with you?"

"I don't feel good," I replied because I was ashamed to tell him the truth.

"You want to come and lay in my bed?"

"Yes."

I still couldn't sleep, hyped up off the effects of the little white pills in my blood stream, so my dad took me for a drive. It was late, but it was what I needed. I cried so hard while looking out of the car window. Thinking, *Is she okay*?

Months passed and then one day, just like that, she was back. I didn't ask questions, I embraced her because I was so happy that she was back.

There were also times when my dad would see the women we encountered during my mother's rage in the old apartment. I can remember doing the woman's two daughters hair. I didn't understand at the time what was going on, or maybe I didn't want to know.

Robbed

One night, Antwan and I were awakened by a flash of lights and the voices of police officers. My mom and dad's room was on the second floor, so as the police officer walked us down to the first floor, I immediately looked in their room.

"Where is my mom?" I asked.

"She's down here," the officer said calmly.

My mom was sitting on the couch, clutching Brandy. When she caught sight of us, she got up and hugged us tightly.

"What 's going on?" I cried, worried by all the surrounding activity.

"Someone broke into your house," the officer said.

I scanned the living room trying to see what had been taken. Then it hit me as I looked over to the empty spot where the big brown floor model television used to be and it was gone. Someone had taken it. That was all we had of value. It was weird though, my sister would normally wake up and want a bottle or something. I know because she was like an alarm clock. But she didn't this time plus my dad had been gone to work at the correctional facility.

When my dad came home, the first thing I remember my mom saying was, "I'm not staying in this house."

"Uh huh," my father mumbled with eyes scanning the living room.

"Are you hearing me?" my mother asked.

"Yes, I heard you and the house is not safe," my father bellowed back.

"We can't stay here, not with three children, and I refuse to go back to live with my mother."

"You don't have to go back and live with her," dad said.

"We're not staying here one more night, you hear me."

"I understand, just give me a second. I need to think."

My dad needed time so he could come up with a plan but my mom was two steps ahead.

"There's nothing to think about. The kids and I are going back to California."

"Ernestine, calm down, you are not moving back."

My mom went up the stairs to pack. My heart broke into a million little pieces, I felt like this was the end. I ran upstairs to my room in tears. And in a blink of an eye, we were back in California. Words could not express how hurt I was.

Our house was robbed that night, but I also felt like I was robbed. I didn't want to leave my dad behind. I knew things would never be the same, and they weren't. My family was falling apart.

The Effect of Being Me

For so many years I struggled with feelings of low self-esteem and unworthiness. The role of a father is to teach his daughter how to be strong, courageous and be in a healthy relationship with a man. In fact, a father is the first relationship a daughter has, and it teaches her how a woman should be treated. But, with my dad being gone, I lacked that role model and would seek to fill that void in other ways, by giving my body to a guy just to feel what I thought was love.

I often settled when it came to finding a partner. I was constantly attracted to the wrong ones. Dads set the standard for their daughters, but without a father, I set my own standards, and I allowed others to define me.

Letter to My Younger Self

Lynnie,

It's ok to say you have daddy issues. To understand them, you must face them and see them for what they are. Remember grandma used to always say call a spade a spade which meant call it how it is, no sugar coating needed and understand that you are not alone.

    I know you feel robbed and have unresolved issues, but I want you to know you can overcome those issues. You must find someone to talk to that you trust and share how you feel. That may be at the church or at school, but the key is to find someone.

    I know losing the bond with dad affected multiple areas of your life, including your emotional life and self-confidence. I know you didn't want to be abandoned again.

    If you don't deal with the trauma of your loss, it will continue to pop up. If you don't deal with these issues, you are beginning a dysfunctional relationship cycle that will damage your self-esteem. You will forego your confidence, power and resilience for pity and low self-worth. Understand that this negative experience can produce positive qualities, such as leadership abilities, resilience, empathy for others, strength in a crisis and unshakable survival skills.

Work and search for your wise self. The pain and confusion you are feeling will go away. Although you've had to make up your own playbook, find examples of people who have thrived in the face of their adversity to make it through. Their experiences will give you strength.

Know that chaos in the home can have a significant impact in every area of your upbringing.

Develop a spirit of determination and survival. Don't accept less in relationships due to lack of self-esteem. You don't have to work for love you have to understand it and show it.

Claim your own journey, your own voice and your own strength as you keep going and move into the stronger chapters of your life. Although you have learned to help yourself, take a deep breath and realize that sometimes it is okay to soften your shell and ask for others to support and understand you.

This does not make you weak, it makes you strong beyond belief. All you need to move forward is the desire for growth and the openness for help.

Faith and healing will show up for you. If you do the work to overcome your challenges, you are on your way to a happy, successful life full of love.

It is okay for you to still experience pain, miss dad and have conflicting emotions such as anger, confusion and neediness. One of the best things you can do to heal is to find a purpose in your pain. Understand that you are on a journey that will grow and change throughout your life just as you will. Be patient with your emotions and know through it all you are growing in wisdom and resilience.

But most importantly of all, remember to always believe in yourself. You can achieve whatever you set your mind to Lynnie. Let no one tell you differently.

Sincerely,

Lynn
Your Future Self

Daddy's Gone Commentary

1 John 4:19 ESV: We love because he first loved us.

When I say you need to love yourself, I'm not referring to the stuck-up, prideful, worldly type of loving oneself. Instead, I'm talking about a concept of being thankful, and appreciating the person who God has made in you. Young ladies, you are wonderfully and beautifully made by the creator. You do not need a man to define who you are or who you are meant to be. Love is not just a word it's an action. God gave us his ONLY Son, Jesus to die on the cross for our sins. That is the perfect example of Love. If someone is not willing to love you like that, then they're not worthy of you. You hold the key. You're unique and designed for a purpose. No one should ever want to dim the light that shines inside of you. Yes, our fathers are the first of everything and I'm sorry to say some fathers don't know the impact they have on us. Just know even if you don't have your father in your life, your heavenly father is always there. I know, I've witnessed it. God is with you. He will never leave you nor forsake you. He loves you that much.

Reflections For Your Journey

✦ Don't let your circumstances dictate your attitude.

✦ Don't let what you think life should be stop you from living in the present moment.

✦ Let go of needless expectations.

✦ Release the pain of rejection and live in the joy of the present.

✦ You can only fight today's battles.

✦ Allow God to control your thoughts rather than your thoughts controlling you.

✦ Don't put your hope in things that will disappoint you.

Lynn Barnes

Journal

Beyond What You See

Lynn Barnes

Chapter Three
My Devil

"For where God built a church, there the Devil would also build a chapel."
~Martin Luther

We moved in with my Aunt and my two cousins, Kala and Darius. Twan and I enjoyed being with them but it wasn't like being in St. Louis with my dad. My mom didn't wait long before dating again. I can remember every relationship and the impact they had on me, but there was one person who would change our lives forever; Donald Schmidt was his name. When he walked through the door, it was like time had stood still for a moment. A strobe light searched the room seeking the right angle to shine on Donald, giving off glimpses of the man that would soon send us further down the spiraling hole that had become my life.

My mom's eyes lit up and her smile was as bright as a toothpaste commercial. If his short afro could have blown in the wind, I was convinced it would have. He had a deep brown complexion, a mustache and thick brows. On the surface, he looked like he had it all together but we would soon see he had a drug problem.

My brother and I looked at my mom then looked at each other as if saying in unison, "We're doomed."

But that was an understatement and in a matter of days we were moving in with him.

Moving to Hell

We knew nothing about this man he could have been a killer for all we knew. One night he took us to this small tan house in Lynwood right outside of Compton.

"Ya'll wait here I will open the door," he said.

So, we waited.

"Mom, why is he going to the back?" I asked.

"He said he has nosy neighbors."

"Oh."

Then the front door opened.

"Ya'll come on!"

So, we got out of the van and walked up to the house. The lights were off and he had candles.

"Why are the lights off?" I asked.

"Stop asking so many questions." my mom snapped back.

There was no furniture and no pictures on the walls. The house was bare. I wanted to ask why, but I didn't want the smack down, so Twan and I rolled with it. My brother walked into the bathroom.

"The toilet's not working either, how am I going to flush?" he asked.

"Oh, just pour some water in the top part," Donald responded.

Lucky for us, the water was about the only thing that was working. My mom made pallets for us on the floor. She took Brandy in the room with her and

Donald. Twan and I laid there for about fifteen to twenty minutes before we realized something,

"Twan, we didn't eat yet," I said.

"I was too disgusted to notice," he responded. I wasn't about to get up and ask either. Morning couldn't come quick enough. I saw Donald dragging a long orange extension cord from outside. I went to the bathroom to wash my face and brush my teeth, yeah, you guessed it. No towels, no toothbrush or toothpaste, because we left ours at my Aunts house. Dare I ask about breakfast, I thought, shoot yeah, I'm hungry.

"Momma! What are we eating?"

My mom was coming out of the bedroom.

"We're going to get some donuts."

"Okay, let me get dressed."

"No, you guys stay here," she replied.

"Why?" I fired back in frustration.

And then she gave me *the stare*. I walked away before a shoe came my way. I feared my mom. She was *true crazy*. You know how there is *maybe crazy;* when you get the look but no action. Then there is *just crazy;* when you get the look and words but no action. Next there's true crazy; that's when you get the look then action but no words. So yeah, I walked away from whatever was coming my way. Twan was still asleep on the floor, so I sat down beside him.

"Twan, momma is getting donuts."

"Oh, cool."

I knew that would wake him up, food always woke him up, especially donuts. So, he laid there for a minute and then got up.

"How long ago did they leave?" He asked.

"About ten minutes ago," I responded.

Ten minutes became two hours and twenty-five minutes. I was looking out the window thinking, *It's a nice sunny day, I wish we could go outside.*

We would get used to this loneliness and waiting on momma. I knew she had been using drugs for some time now, but I didn't realize how bad it would get. Soon I saw Donald's big blue van pull up.

"They're here!" I said.

Twan ran to the window.

"It's about time," he responded.

They walked through the door with two to three plastic bags of groceries a piece. I did not understand what they had to go through to get those groceries and I didn't care. I acted like I was helping, but I was just looking for the donuts and milk. She pulled out paper plates, cups, spoon, forks, soap, face towels, cleaning supplies and, a box of mixed donuts, you know the ones with powdered, chocolate and coconut. They were all so good, but the coconut were my favorite.

No Stability
Right before school started, my mom told us we would move into another house.

"Momma, why are we moving again?"

"Lynnie look, we have to move baby, I know we keep having to move and I'm sorry, but once we move this time, we won't have to for a while... hopefully."

But I wasn't convinced and rightfully so. I soon realized that my mom's new boyfriend, was squatting; breaking into vacant houses and moving us in. It all made since now. That's why the houses were bare and nothing worked and that's also why I saw the long orange cord. Mr. Gadget aka Donald was stealing electricity from the neighbors. So, we moved into yet another free property. This went on for over three months. We would move, go to school like everything was hunky dory and then once we got caught, we would move again. I was tired and scared because I didn't want us to go to jail. Well, I wanted Donald to go to jail for life, but I wanted nothing to happen to my mom, Twan and I.

The Hustle

Donald started silk screening poems. He said he wrote them, but we didn't believe him. So, every time we'd moved we also had to move his big heavy wooden contraption of junk and cans of blue paint.

Donald got us to work selling his stupid posters. He would drop us off at a grocery store or a corner with no training involved. Our first time out Twan was scared; He didn't know how to approach total strangers let alone ask them for money, but neither did I.

"I can't do this," he said.

"Look Twan, do you want to eat?"

"Yes."

"Okay, I'll go first."

So, I walked up to a tall well-dressed white man.

"Excuse me sir, we are selling posters. Would you like to buy one?"

The guy looked hesitant but replied by asking to see them.

"The big ones are ten-dollars; the mediums are five-dollars and the small ones are a dollar." I said.

"Here you go," the man said, handing me a twenty-dollar bill.

"Which one would you like?" I said.

"None," then he walked away.

Twan and I looked at each other with the biggest smiles on our faces. Not because we made a sale, but because we didn't. Meaning we still had inventory, but we also had money.

"Twan, let's eat."

With a big Kool-Aid smile on his face and a shake of his head he said, "C'mon!"

We ran to the nearest burger joint. We ended up selling posters that day, but at least we did it on a full stomach. Donald picked us up about three hours later.

"How many did you guys sell?" Donald asked.

"Two big ones and five small ones,"

"That's all?"

"You got to do better than that."

Twan and I looked at each other and smirked as we both thought, *If only you knew*.

Over the next few months, Donald made it his business for us to be better at selling his posters of poems. On the days we didn't have posters to sell, we would sell coupon books. It became routine. It almost became fun because Twan and I would see who could sell the most. We learned the hustle.

The Hustle: To proceed or work rapidly or energetically; to push or force one's way.

When we could not sell posters, we resulted to stealing. My mother picked up Bran and put her in the stroller with her baby blanket and diaper bag at the bottom of the stroller. We roamed through the grocery store adding food to the bottom of the stroller and covered it up with Bran's blanket. My mother always grabbed a bottle of ketchup to buy because we couldn't just walk out with the merchandise or we would look suspicious. I learned the five-finger discount early on and got good at it, although I knew it was wrong. I liked to eat, but didn't get to do it often, so this way I could. This started my downward spiral into taking things that didn't belong to me. It became a way for me to have what I didn't and that was something to fill my stomach. This was another reason I hated Donald and everything about him.

A Toxic Environment
Their relationship made little sense. The occasional arguments over the lack of food and not having a stable place to live made our environment toxic. I remember my brother and I arguing over a spoon and

fork when the unthinkable happened. Smack! Right across my face.

"Why did you hit me?" I screamed.

I knew my brother didn't mean it. We were in a hostile environment and were adapting to it. "Sis I'm sorry, I didn't mean too."

I knew we had to leave. Donald was beating on my mom every chance he could and it was only a matter of time before he came after us. I had only seen my dad hit my mom twice, but I would later find out there were many more times she remembers. So why was it so easy for her to leave my dad but not Donald? She had changed, and I didn't like this new woman. I was always sure that my mom would stomp a hole in our back side, but she never allowed anyone else to touch us. Now, I wasn't so sure of that.

One night, while we were outside, Donald was yelling at my mom.

It looked like he was getting ready to hit her when out of nowhere my big brother Twan ran over to him, "Don't you touch her! If you hit her again, I will kill you!" He screamed.

I knew this would be the moment Donald would back down and leave or my mom would see that this was tearing us apart. Instead of that happening, Donald walked up to my brother and punched him in the face. My mom and I froze as we watched my brother fall to the ground.

I ran over to Twan.

"Are you okay?" I screamed.

"Leave me alone!" my brother said as he looked at my mom get smacked and kicked.

I looked around for help but it was like time stopped for everyone else but us and no one was around.

My brother was fed up. "I'm leaving and going back to St. Louis with dad!"

"Well, you're not leaving me here, I'm going with you," I added.

The Effect of Being Me

I hated selling posters and coupon books. I was embarrassed. It felt like we were begging. I was influenced by my view of the world, my family, friends, and the things I experienced. We squatted in homes and went without eating for days at a time. I found myself second guessing my mom and who she had become. This was taking a toll on me and my brother. We made each other laugh and made up fun ways selling posters on the street corner. So, it was out of character for him to hit me. He loved me too much. It wasn't him in that moment, it was the hunger, fear and being pissed off every day. So, I forgave him and hugged him back even tighter. Antwan gave me strength and courage. He was my rock. I felt so helpless when I couldn't help my brother. I froze when I should have gone after Donald too. My brother was my protector. Donald may have weakened my mom, but he never broke us down.

Lynn Barnes

Letter to My Younger Self

Lynnie,

Stop re-experience and reliving the resentment you feel for Donald in your mind. True, you've been affected emotionally, physiologically, and spiritually in very destructive ways. But know that the resentment that you feel is the most devastating block to repairing the connections you value. Your strong reaction of resentment isn't warranted by what sets it off. It's the product of a long history of backed-up unhappiness. The unhappiness that brings the resentment comes from, what we feel people did to you that was hurtful and I know you feel you hold both your mom and Donald responsible for that. I also know you hold the people in your life who did not do what we feel they should have done.

When you hold on to resentment you are refusing to forgive and let bygones be bygones. We review and rehash our painful past, even as we profess to want to let go of it. We do so because we believe the illusion that by holding on to our resentment, we will somehow achieve the justice we believe we are due. We cling to a need to be *right*, which overrides the capacity to heal and be at peace with ourselves.

To move past this, you must: release the resentment that you are feeling because it brings no value to your life and only hurts you. Acknowledge that you cannot change the past and understand that your resentment gives you only illusions of strength. Instead, highlight and validate your real strength and power.

You have a strength inside of you that will help you on your journey, you must hold tight and lean on the father that is present…Your Heavenly Father.

You must also learn to identify signals that trigger resentment and practice putting thoughts between your feelings of resentment and playing them back in your mind. You were broken but the pieces can be put back together even stronger than they were before.

Sincerely,

Lynn
Your Future Self

My Devil Commentary

Ephesians 6:11: Put on the whole armor of God, that you may be able to stand against the schemes of the devil.

It was not my brothers place to fight Donald. An eleven-year-old should never be in that position, but as children we are innocent and our hearts are genuine. To Twan it was the right thing to do. My mother should have protected us. We were the children, and they were the adults. Wondering if we would go to jail for breaking into a home or when we would eat should have never been. I remember a stronger more protective person than what I was seeing now. This was not my mom. It was more like an empty shell. I encourage every parent to meet the needs of your child. Don't let them go through unnecessary adult issues that's not their burden. Be the adult and let them be kids. Take care of them for they are a precious gift from God.

Psalm 127:3 NLT Children are a gift from the Lord; they are a reward from him.

Reflections For Your Journey

- ✦ Call on the name of the Lord and ask Him for help.

- ✦ Trust God to protect you.

- ✦ Don't feel you must be the hero.

- ✦ Get familiar with God's word.

- ✦ Remind yourself that you are not what happens to you.

- ✦ Practice forgiveness.

- ✦ Start an open dialog with your parents.

Lynn Barnes

Journal

Beyond What You See

Lynn Barnes

Chapter Four

Broken

"Loneliness and the feeling of being unwanted is the most terrible poverty."
~Mother Teresa

We took the train to St. Louis as I contemplated how to persuade my dad to let me stay with Twan. I didn't want to go back to California. Who in their right mind wanted to return to hell?

When we arrived in St. Louis, we went to my grandmother's house to wait for my dad to come pick up Twan. I had prepared my plea in my head and was ready when he arrived. My dad pulled up to the house. My heart was beating out of my chest.

"Daddy!" I yelled with excitement and fear wrapped up in one.

"Hey baby."

"Daddy can I please stay with you!" I cried.

I needed my dad in my life for stability, and I yearned for his love. All I wanted him to do was grab me in his arms and hold me close so I could hear him speak through his chest.

"Listen Sweetie, you really need to stay with your mom, she needs you and you need her."

"Daddy please I want to stay with you," I begged.

"Nah you really need to stay with your mom".

I was heartbroken and angry. I wasn't thinking about what my mother needed because she wasn't thinking about what I needed. My mom decided not to leave right away so there was still a chance to convince my dad I needed to be with him. My mom stayed with my grandmother while I went with my dad and Twan. We drove to a complex called The Village. It was the summer, so the kids were out and the water hydrants were flowing. As I walked into the cozy two-bedroom apartment, I couldn't help but notice a huge family portrait of my dad, the woman from the old apartment and her two daughters. Is this why he didn't want me to stay with him? Were they a family now? I was fuming I couldn't breathe. This woman keeps popping up. Why? I felt robbed all over again. This is MY dad, MINE! I wasn't about to let them take him without a fight. I ended up staying for the summer but it came with a price. My dad's girlfriend didn't like my brother and I, nor did her two daughters.

I remember them taking their clothes and throwing them out of the room screaming, "Why are you doing that?"

"Stop throwing our stuff!" They shouted.

At first, I thought, *these kids are crazy*. But then I realized they were trying to get me in trouble and it was working. My dad got on me every time they did things like that. They got away with murder, and I always took the wrap. Over the next month, I stayed to myself. I made sure I stayed out of the wicked step sisters' way, but that didn't keep my dad's girlfriend from coming after me.

One night she told me to take a bath. I ran the water and sat in the tub for about thirty minutes then got out. Taking bird bathes were common for me so I washed up out of the sink. I got dressed then walked out to the living room. She quickly walked to the bathroom.

"Lynn come here," she summonsed.

"Yes," I replied.

"I told you to take a bath."

"I did."

"No, you didn't. Get in the tub and take a bath with your nasty self."

So, I got back in the tub and sat there wondering why I had to do this all over again. I missed my mom, but I didn't want to go back to California. Twan met some kids in the neighborhood so he wasn't home much. I also found an outlet, selling penny candy, cookies and pickles on the ice cream truck. It was fun and a way to stay busy and out of trouble. I couldn't help but think of my mom though. I needed her in the worst way. I didn't want to leave, but I didn't want to stay where I wasn't wanted. The summer came to an end and so I made the choice to go back with my mom. I was torn because I was leaving my dad and not the other way around. I needed him, but I also needed my brother. Twan was my best friend, and I didn't want to be without him. We had gone through so much together and this would be the first time we were apart. It was like separating twins. What would I do?

Broken, I thought about everything I had experienced: the neglect, the abuse and the impoverished lifestyle we had been living. Crying uncontrollably was the only way for me to cope because I didn't want that life. Living in abandoned houses was something I didn't want anymore. Hunger, watching my mother get beat, taking beatings myself, I was done. I didn't know when I would even get a chance to talk to Twan again. There weren't cell phones back then, and we didn't have a house phone. I was only twelve, and I felt like I made the biggest mistake of my life.

I didn't have my father emotionally, or physically. I felt incomplete, going through the motions in my personal hell and the devil wasn't far. It's difficult to show love from over 1,800 miles away, which was the distance between us for most of my childhood.

Everything seemed so complicated. My father had a new family, and I felt neglected, like an afterthought. I didn't feel I was his baby girl, instead I was a burden. My father didn't fight to have a relationship with me.

I became angrier and angrier, an emotion so much easier to live with than hurt. Although it wasn't true, I believed my father never thought of me. I wanted him to want me.

Mom and I returned home to California and the train ride seemed to last for an eternity. I was distraught because I was missing Twan and it felt unbearable not having him by my side. I tried to mentally prepare myself to return to the situation that was my life. When we returned Donald had found a new house for us to squat. It was still summer in California and it was hot. I remember this house vividly because mom met a friend named Linda who lived in the apartment complex down the block. I remember Linda because she was strung out on heroin.

Linda had a daughter named Netta and we became friends. Netta was a fast tail little girl. We were twelve, and she had a boyfriend. It was easy for her to get away with anything because like me she was raising herself along with her little brother Ronnie who was two-years-old. Ronnie was one of the most hyper kids I had ever seen. He jumped off of banisters, chairs, porches or whatever he could find. I figured it was the effects of being born to a drug-addicted mother. Now Ronnie was paying the price or rather Netta was since she handled him. Most of the conversations Netta and I had were about boys. I had no experience with boys, but she was a wealth of information. She was more experienced than any twelve-year-old should have been.

I remember my mom leaving us often to go to Linda's house. One day Bran and I were home alone, and I noticed that mom was much longer than usual. Bran was sleep, so I went to find my mom. As I headed down the street, I saw a lot of commotion going on at Linda's house. I didn't know what was happening until I saw Linda foaming at the mouth and my mother was trying to sit her up to help her.

I stood at the doorway in amazement watching Linda's lifeless body on the floor as my mom tried to revive her. Linda was dying, and it scared me. It scared me because my mom was on drugs too. All I could think about was my mom in that same position, foaming at the mouth.

As soon as my mother got Linda stable, she turned to me and hollered, "Where is Bran!"

I left Bran home alone and my mom was furious. Although I was still in shock from the fact that I had just seen my mom was focused on the fact I had left my baby sister.

After that my mom never spoke about what happened. She asked if I was ok, but that was it. Traumatized, I had to cope, which was to just keep going. There was no comfort from my mom, no hugs or checking my mental state. It was just over and never to be mentioned again.

Since we never stayed in one place too long, it would be three months before we were moving never to see Linda and Netta again. The constant site of transition became the norm, and I always knew the friends I met were temporary. But that didn't stop me from hoping one day we would stop moving and I could experience the stability I had been missing.

Lynn Barnes

The Effect of Being Me

I was a girl raised without a father, plagued by low self-esteem plus an unreliable sense of self. I internalized this into my own messed up patterns and made mistakes.

After leaving my brother, I was an empty shell and disconnected. My confidant was no longer around to help me cope with the daily madness of my life. My support system and comic relief was gone so smiles were few.

My mother's drug use was the backdrop to my childhood. Everything my brother and I went through centered on it. Relaxing for me was impossible. I'm always eager to be in control. I find it hard to trust other people. For so long, I felt threatened because of the insecurities I harbored. I associated closeness with unpredictability and, even worse, unbearable responsibility.

Like most children of drug addicts, I grew up long before my time, becoming a mother to both my sister and myself. My mother was absent even when she was present. I could not rely on or confide my problems in her.

Witnessing so much at a young age put unbearable pressure on me. Worried about my mother, I was sad and scared the same things I saw with Linda would happen to my mom. My young mind could not separate what I had seen from what might occur. I knew my mom did crack, but I didn't know what else she was using and I was scared for us. If something happened to my mother Donald would be the only one person to take care of us. This made me develop anxieties and abandonment issues. I wanted my life to be normal, but I did not understand what that even looked like.

Lynn Barnes

Letter to My Younger Self

Lynnie,

Your dad loves you. He may not know how to show it and his hands are tied because he knows your mother needs you. You may have lost Twan, but he is still your brother and will be there for you always. Use this time to get to know yourself. Explore who you are and what you want out of life.

You were not robbed, things just changed in life. It may seem unfair, but it was best for Twan to have that strong male influence in his life. Understand that you have a unique perspective. You are lucky to be a part of an inseparable unit. Having Twan in your life enriched you and helped to give you inner strength.

Don't allow fear to consume you as it relates to mom. You must give it to God because it's not your burden to bear. You must pray and ask God to heal her, but release the fear that something will happen to her. She is an adult who makes her own decisions and there is nothing you can do about it.

Your childhood is making you strong to prepare you for the rest of your life. You will overcome the feelings you have but you must keep a level head. Release the anger and hatred in your heart so it doesn't affect the rest of your life. Don't allow her disease to stop you from being who God created you to be.

Remember that who you are is on you; your parents are not responsible for your decisions. Although the first part of your life has been challenging, one day you will look back and reflect to see that God was with you for the entire journey.

You are a child of God which makes you an heir with Christ, meaning you are entitled to all that God had to give to His own Child, so don't hate life, embrace it.

Sincerely,

Lynn
Your Future Self

Lynn Barnes

Being Broken Commentary

> *Psalm 34:18 NIV The LORD is near to the brokenhearted and saves those who are crushed in spirit.*

The Lord is near to the broken hearted. Near in friendship to accept and console. Broken hearts think God is far away when he is most near to them; their eyes are closed so they don't see their best friend. He is with them, and in them, but they know it not. What a blessed token for good is a mourning heart! Just when the sinner condemns himself, the Lord graciously absolves him. If we chasten our own spirits, the Lord will spare us. He never breaks with the rod of judgment to those who are already sore with the rod of conviction. Salvation is linked with contrition.

Reflections For Your Journey

- Know you are not alone.

- Believe God is working on your behalf through your adversities.

- Know your life will serve as a testament to others.

- Your broken heart will be healed by God if you allow Him to.

- Don't be consumed by fear.

- Use your experiences to grow.

- You have the power to change your life.

Lynn Barnes

Journal

Beyond What You See

Lynn Barnes

Chapter Five
I Was Lost

"Always remember that your present situation is not your final destination. The best is yet to come."
~Lynn Barnes

Once again I was headed to a new school. I had more first days of school than a class full of first graders. It was the middle of the school year by the time we found a new place, and all I could think about was possibly getting school clothes and my hair done.

"Mom, will I get school clothes this year?"

"We'll see," mom said.

That meant no, because I heard that before. So I ended up wearing maternity clothes from the Goodwill. I had two shirts, one pair of pants and one pair of socks to carry me through the rest of the school year. It would take creativity and a miracle to make those things look good.

As the first day of school approached, my mom found a lady to relax my hair. When I woke up the next morning all my hair had fallen out. Now I had a short afro and maternity clothes resembling a militant mother.

The day before school started, I was able to get a Jeri Curl which was a small improvement when it wasn't dry, but it was. I looked like a boy. I could have been my brother's twin and others thought so too.

There I was, standing in front of the mirror.

"This is bad," I said to my reflection.

I grabbed the rest of the trial size activator that came with the Curl kit, put it on my hands then rubbed it in to my hair as best as I could but it wasn't enough. After I put my clothes on, I felt disgusted.

There were beads of sweat and the drippings of my curl juice racing down the sides of my face.

It felt like a bad dream I couldn't wake up from and now on top of my hair nightmare, Donald was taking me to school for the first time.

"You ready to go?" asked Donald.

I wanted to say no so bad, but I knew it wouldn't have made a difference.

"Yeah, I guess."

We got into the van and went. I can remember getting into 'Big Blue' the name we had given his van that often smelled like marijuana and trash. There were no seat belts and I didn't like riding in it. The ride was silent besides the morning talk radio that served as background noise. A few blocks from the school, Donald made a sharp turn and I slid towards the door. To my surprise the door swung open and I went falling. But right before I slid out the door, I felt a force grab my short afro and yanked me back inside the vehicle.

I was in shock, not because I almost died, but why pull my hair when he had so many other choices, like my arm or my jacket? Well, I believe it's because he was an evil addict that was ushering my family into hell. I couldn't wait to get out of the blue death trap.

When we pulled up to the junior high school, I jumped out of the van. Walking through the breezeway into the courtyard felt surreal because I was going to school for the first time without my brother. The one person who made it bearable to be the new kid. The only person who would protect me against the laughing and pointing of ignorant people. I wanted to turn around and walk right back out of the doors.

The thought of Donald picking me up from school wasn't pleasant, and before I knew it, the day was over. I waited in the front of the school for him to pick me up.

I waited for what seemed like an eternity, and Donald was nowhere in sight. Soon, I was the last one standing. It was boiling hot that day and I remember not being able to find shade. The longer I stood there it became more clear he wasn't coming. I got tired of waiting, so I walked home. I walked down the street we drove from, trying to recall landmarks.

"Okay, I think I turn here," I mumbled.

At first, things looked familiar, but soon they no longer resembled anything I remembered. I turned down an alleyway and walked past some men playing dice. My heart was pounding so hard in my chest I thought they would hear it, but the men didn't even notice me.

I passed the prostitutes selling their bodies and the drug dealers selling their dope. After walking another few blocks, I came to terms with the fact that I was lost. While I continued to walk slowly, I knew I had to make a decision. I debated if I should continue to walk in the same direction and turn the upcoming corner or just turn around and go back the way I came. It was getting dark and I had walked over twenty blocks. At that moment, I stopped in my tracks.

"Go the way you came," I heard a still voice say.

No one was around, but I felt a sense of comfort come over me. I felt God was with me. The decision was clear. I did what the voice said and went back in the direction I had come from.

Now it was dark and I had been walking for hours. Finally, I could see the school in the distance along with the blue and red flashing lights of a police car.

"There she is!" I heard my mother yell.

"Lynnie!"

Normally I would run the other way, but not this time. This time, I ran as fast as I could right into her arms.

Could God Hear Me?

That Sunday, I put on the Easter dress mom purchased the previous year and went to church by myself. There was a local church bus that always came to the neighborhood to pick up people for church, so when I saw it, I asked if I could go. I had five dollars, and I put it in the offering basket. There was so much on my mind after that.

I would look up and ask, "If you are really God, why am I going through this?"

I didn't get an answer which made me think God couldn't even hear me.

Little did I know, He was refining me. Being lost in an unfamiliar place was frightening. I felt like a stranger in a strange land lacking any clues that could help me find myself. We moved over ten times while I was growing up, so unfamiliar became second nature. Lack of stability contributed to my uncertainty, stuck roaming around trying to find my way back to something familiar.

It wasn't long before we were found out. When I saw the police car, I knew it was a problem. They came to evict us from the house we were squatting in for the past month. They caught us in the house, so there wasn't much Donald could say. You see, there was an art to squatting and Donald had mastered it. If we weren't home when the police came, they would come back. If we were home and Donald told them we lived there, it would take thirty days to get us out. This time when they came we had to get out immediately. We were being displaced once again, which had become the norm. I could not get used to it.

It was hard not having stability in my life and never knowing if I would have a place to sleep.

I lost my dad, my brother, got lost in a strange neighborhood and now I had lost another piece of my security being kicked out of another house. I didn't know what was going on or where we would land. I felt terrible and wanted to be anywhere but there.

The Effect of Being Me

There was a change taking place in my character. As time went by, I felt inferior to everyone and it made me hate myself. I did not know what to do with my life — and I was starting to not even care. I was craving connection, and looking for specific experiences and people to satisfy them, but I was isolating myself. This caused the moments of happiness to be few and far between.

The more I experienced and explored my own feelings of uncertainty and loneliness, the more I realized how necessary these feelings are. It's good for us to explore the unknowns alone. It gives us an opportunity to discover who we are and what life is about.

You must be lost first to find what you're looking for. Until you are lost in this world you can't find your best path. Realizing you are lost is the first step to living the life you want. The second step is letting go of the life you don't want.

Everyone feels lost sometimes. When you apply what you're learning to your future choices and actions, you move forward not backwards. You become stronger and wiser. It's difficult, but it's worth it.

I didn't know where I was going or how I got to where I was. I didn't have people around me who knew either. I had to ask myself who I was on the inside because my outside was broken. I handled situations based on patterns learned in childhood allowing the past to control me. I didn't create a set of principles to follow or live by so the lines of right and wrong often blurred. Witnessing so much at a young age put unbearable pressure on me. I was being someone else other than who God created me to be.

Letter to My Younger Self

Lynnie,

Think about where you want to go in life. The bottom line is, it comes down to what you think about yourself. There will be obstacles, but you have the power to overcome them. Even though they seem insurmountable, you can conquer them. Let no one or anything discourage you from continuing on. Believe in yourself and believe in your decisions.

Block out the negativity from yourself and other people. Silence the voice in your head that tells you that you aren't good enough and asked yourself what would make you happy. Once you know, you pursue that thing by any means necessary.

Stay positive and keep moving forward. You don't have to have it all figured out to move forward. Sometimes, just taking one step can show you the staircase to the door you've been searching for. It doesn't take some big plan to live a happy life. It takes following your heart and making decisions rather than waiting for the perfect answer to appear. Add meaning to your life, by taking part in activities you feel are important.

Remember to talk out your feelings rather than acting them out. When you act first, the consequences are usually negative.

When you feel lost in life, just remember what you've learned from your past, and keep your eyes focused ahead on all the good things awaiting you.

Remember, if you hit a roadblock, you can always turn around and find a different way. There are many paths to take in life, and you might look for the one that's right for you. Take your time and don't rush your destiny.

Your childhood is making you strong to prepare you for the rest of your life. You will overcome the feelings you have but you must keep a level head. Release the anger and hatred in your heart so it doesn't affect the rest of your life. Don't allow your mother's disease to stop you from being who God created you to be.

Sometimes, feeling lost in life just means you haven't had enough time to connect with yourself. Sitting in silence, reflecting, listening to music or praying to escape the noise of life can provide clarity. Remember to pay attention to what you hear in the silence. Quiet your inner world and you'll find what you need.

Because you have lived through so much, endured many hardships, life has hardened you and caused you to become closed off from the world. Life does not come with a rule book or deadlines for accomplishing certain things. To find your path, follow your intuition, and never give up. Stay persistent and don't allow negative thinking to pull you in. In the past I felt like I needed to be at the same level as everyone else my age, but life is not a race or a contest.

Have faith because you are where you need to be at this moment in time. As long as your content, don't allow anyone to convince you that you're not where you need to be. You be the judge of what you want to change in your life and then do it for you.

Sincerely,

Lynn

Your Future Self

Lynn Barnes

Being Broken Commentary

Psalm 25:16-17: Turn to me and be gracious to me, for I am lonely and afflicted. Relieve the troubles of my heart and free me from my anguish.

Jesus never said the road would be easy. He shared the ways the world would affect us, and the trouble we would face as Christians. God knew we would struggle to hold on to him in a world with so many challenges. When we face feelings of emptiness, it is because our hearts have grown heavy due to what we're experiencing in life. When we feel lost, it is because we have allowed that heaviness to keep us stuck and stops us from seeking Jesus to remove the burdens we face. This scripture is a reminder that Jesus knows and understands the challenges we face. He knows the world and has overcome it and he can help us do the same.

    God turns to us, no matter who turns from us. God has taught us that without Him we can do nothing. He shows us the way to lift our whole hearts and desires to Him. He is our righteousness. There is not a feeling we can have that God is not aware. He knows when we are hurting, lost, lonely, and afraid. When we cry out to him in our pain, he responds tenderly. While our troubles may not go away, his loving response to our prayers can help us face them with renewed strength. He placed within us a piece of himself...a reminder we are not alone. When emptiness threatens to fall upon you, look inward to the place where the Lord lives. Strength lies there, with Him.

Reflections For Your Journey

+ Spend time exploring your thoughts.

+ Know that the journey won't be easy, but it's worth it.

+ Realize that you can do nothing without God.

+ Feeling lost is the first step to finding yourself.

+ Create a standard for your life.

+ Don't be scared to turn around and change your direction.

+ Believe in yourself and believe in your decisions.

Beyond What You See

Journal

Lynn Barnes

Chapter Six
Alone & Unwanted

"I'm falling apart right before your eyes but you don't see me."
~Invisible

As the cycle of my so-called life continued, once again we were homeless. We moved in with my Aunt Sherrie and my cousins in Compton. I hadn't seen them in a long time and I missed them. Things were different. It wasn't us four anymore since Twan was in St. Louis with dad. Now it was just Kayla, Darius and I. Kayla had her friends and Darius had his friends. I was trying to fit in where I could. I still have great memories of the fun we had. Some days, Kayla and I would go over to the Compton Court building, which was at the corner of our block where we would play in the parking garage. We would act like some kind of special agents being chased by spies. We would see a car coming and dodge behind a parked car.

"Did they see us?"

"No, I don't think so."

"Let's go!"

We would run and stand against the big white round pillars. We would sing the famous theme song from *The Six Million Dollar Man*. I love this memory. Kayla and I were like sisters. My grams used to buy us the same clothes so we could dress alike. We had been close, but again, things were different somehow. We got into arguments. Then we'd end up not speaking to one another for days and I hated that. I wasn't used to it. But when we got over it and were on speaking terms again, we had the best times. One time, Kayla put salt in Darius hair while he was sleep.

Now that was hilarious to us, but not to Darius. See, he had a Jeri Curl and his hair was nice and thick. When he saw the salt, he thought it was dandruff at first. Kayla and I were crouched down behind the corner wall looking on as he continued to swipe his hand across his curls. Every time he did, it sounded like rain. We laughed so hard.

One night, while laying on my pallet on the floor, my cousin Darius came into the room.

"Hey Lynnie, I'm going to sleep in here."

"Where am I going to sleep?"

"You can stay in here."

"Oh okay."

I wasn't sure if it was okay. I mean this was my cousin Darius. I loved him. This is the one who did hilarious rap remixes, wrote skits for us to perform when we were bored and could make you laugh about anything. So, no worries, this was okay, so I thought. Later that night, I was awakened by Darius' manhood in my face. I didn't know what to do. *Is this all I'm here on this earth for?* I thought. My dad doesn't want me, my mom is coo-coo for cocoa puffs over Donald and now this. At twelve-years-old, I was molested again and I hated myself. Why is this happening to me?

Why Doesn't Anyone Love Me?

I needed my brother. My feelings of self-worth were diminishing more and more every day. I didn't want to look in the mirror and see this person I didn't recognize. I didn't have any more tears to shed. I was an empty shell. I started filling myself up with anger and bitterness. I became hard inside. I felt like I could kill myself or someone else.

We finally ended up at Donald's cousin JoJo's house in Long Beach. JoJo was a crack head and lived there with his girlfriend Audrey. I never saw anyone smoke crack until we moved in with them. This was also when I saw my mom smoke crack for the first time. I knew she was on it, but it wasn't real to me until that moment I saw her holding the pipe up to her lips to smoke. The beatings became worse for my mom while staying there. Even Audrey got beat by Jo Jo. One night, it got so bad that Donald chased my mom down and choked her. I saw her body go limp.

I ran over to her screaming in a panic.

"No! Momma!"

It seemed like it took forever to get to her. I kneeled beside her and held her, but I didn't even check to see if she was dead or not.

"Momma, mommy!" I said as I rocked her.

"I'm okay," she replied in a whispering voice.

As she sat there and caught her breath, I ran to a pay phone to call my dad.

"Hello," a deep voice said on the other end.

"Daddy?"

"No, this is Twan."

"Twan!"

First I had to get over the initial shock of the deep voice, then the excitement came over me actually hearing my brother.

"I need to talk to daddy."

"Why, what's wrong?"

"Donald just tried to kill momma!"

"Dad!"

My dad gets on the phone, "Hello."

"Daddy, can you send for us?"

"What's wrong?"

"Donald just tried to kill momma."

"What!"

"Where is she?"

"She's over on the grass, he ran after her and when he caught up to her, he grabbed her by the neck and started choking her until she fell."

"Daddy, please send for us!" I begged.

"Sweetie... [I'm going to stop right here]. The reason being is because, I knew when my dad called me sweetie, it either meant, I had done something wrong or the answer was *no*. And in this case, well let me just say, after that phone call, I hated my dad. Days later, we moved from Jo Jo's apartment to a two-bedroom house in Long Beach.

The Effect of Being Me

During my period of low self-esteem and extreme uncertainty, I questioned every aspect of my life. I would go to bed frustrated and upset and ask myself, *Is this all I'm good for?* I felt I wasn't good enough, and for the first time I felt like less than nothing.

"Why me?" was a constant thought.

They took my body away from me, so I felt helpless. This thinking was hard to let go. I was looking at everything that was wrong, instead of looking to the Lord for comfort. The bigger part of my unhappiness was due to my circumstances which dictated my attitude and often my actions. The things I was experiencing were causing me pain because I was holding on to them. Negative memories of molestation and abuse were haunting me.

I was afraid and felt alone. I lost hope and felt like I was living in hell and happiness was nowhere in sight. I was becoming confused about life. Why were these things happening to me? Why did we live so poor? Why can't my momma leave these drugs alone and why was I being molested?

Letter to My Younger Self

Lynnie,

The things that were supposed to teach and help you grow caused you pain instead. I wish I could go back in time and hold you myself. Unhappy and hurtful past events brought heartache, depression, and destructive behavior into your life.

The un-forgiveness is bringing bondage into your life. If God forgot our sins for His sake, then I think you ought to do the same for yourself and others, which frees you.

Accept the reality of what is. You cannot find peace by avoiding life. Life spins with unexpected changes; so instead of avoiding it, take every change and experience it as a challenge for growth. Either it will give you what you want or it will teach you the next steps.

Finding peace in life does not mean being in a place where there is no noise, no challenges, and no hard work. It means to be in the midst of those things while remaining calm in your heart. Don't trust every thought that appears in your mind. That is leaning on your own understanding. Trust in the Lord. Allow Him to take the wheel. Don't allow your thoughts to control you.

God never said it would be easy. You may cry, feel confused and experience hurt. I know that it hurts because I had to let go of doing my will. Everyone you care about does NOT need to support your decisions. Friends and family won't always support your goals, but you must pursue them anyway.

Follow your intuition. Following your intuition means doing what feels right, even if it doesn't look or sound right to others. Only time will tell, but our human instincts are rarely wrong. Even if things don't turn out as you expected, at least you won't have to spend the rest of your life wondering what could have been. So, don't worry about what everyone else thinks; just keep living and speaking your truth.

You'll know you're on the right track in life when you become uninterested in looking back and eager to take the next step, regardless of what anyone else thinks.

No one understands the pain you are feeling except for you and God. That is why you must bring your pain to Him. Sometimes the pain hurts so much that you can't even speak.

Speak with your heart and say, "God, help me!" God knows the disappointment, frustration, the pain, and the worry.

Sometimes you have to cry out for this special peace He gives in prayer to help you cope with the situation. It is this special peace that has given me a sound mind and contentment in my situation time and time again. It is like Jesus is giving you an everlasting hug that helps you recover.

Like a good father, He lets you know everything will be ok. God allows these situations to build us up, help us grow in faith, and prepare us for something better. Don't let the past haunt you or be a cloud that hangs over your everyday life. Every time you recall your past unhappiness you bring it to life again and all those old feelings come back to haunt you.

Life is too short to spend at war with yourself. The biggest disappointments in our lives are often the result of misplaced expectations. Releasing needless expectations is your first step to happiness. Come from a mindset of peace and acceptance, and you can deal with almost anything and grow beyond it.

Sincerely,

Lynn

Your Future Self

Alone & Unwanted Commentary

> Isaiah 43:18: *"But forget all that–it is nothing compared to what I am going to do."*

Sometimes we hold on to things such as, unhealthy relationships, negative memories and thoughts and doing our own will because we think things will change. We still hold on to hope in things other than God. We put our hope in things that will always disappoint.

Do not dwell on things from the past because there is more at stake. Dwelling on the past is not wrong, but we must know when to and when not to. The past has many great testimonies of God and His mighty acts, but our lives can't stop there. Did you ever meet someone who always says what great things God did (such as saving him) but never says what great things God is doing for us now? God is not saying that the past things are unimportant but only that He is the Living God and lives to make a difference every day of our lives.

God delights in doing something new. Even more, God delights in involving us in His new plans. The *new* are things which often make us uncomfortable. They lead us to unseen circumstances. We are not sure on how to handle the things which we face. This alone makes it hard. If we stay in the past we get prideful. But these new experiences are always humbling. God stretches us.

Reflections For Your Journey

✦ Don't let things that hurt you take control over you.

✦ Cast your worries in Gods hands, He is waiting with open arms.

✦ Release what you are holding on to. Hurt will only consume you.

✦ You are beautiful in every way. Don't forget who created you and why.

✦ Allow God to show you his unconditional love.

✦ Don't worry about what other people think. You have a purpose in this world.

✦ Don't fear, remember life is a journey and each experience is an opportunity for growth.

Lynn Barnes

Journal

Beyond What You See

Lynn Barnes

Chapter Seven
This Can't Be Life

"Hope is the magic carpet that transports us from the present moment into the realm of infinite possibilities."
~H. Jackson Brown Jr

I was becoming more and more confused, angry and eventually bitter. We moved from Long Beach to a trailer park in El Segundo California with Donald.

My mom and I went to the trailer park one day to get the keys. We walked in and I almost vomited.

The smell alone made my stomach turn. As we tip-toed through dog feces and trash, my mom said, "This isn't so bad."

What! I thought, because I wouldn't dare say it aloud and end up being knocked down. *Not so bad! ... Not so bad!* If I could have stood up to my mom in that moment, I would have won. I was angry and disgusted.

"Let's go," she said.

"Yes, let's," I happily responded.

"We need to get some cleaning supplies."

"Ma, we are cleaning this?"

"Yeah."

"Why do we have to clean it?"

"Because the landlord is giving it to us for cheap if we clean it."

I was done. I believed the boogie man must have killed me the night he violated me. That was the only thing that made sense to me, it was my hell.

After getting the supplies, we came back to the trailer to start cleaning. As we started, I noticed deep scratch marks on the walls.

"Ma, look!" I exclaimed.

My mom came over to where I was standing.

"Oh, the guy said the people who were here last locked the dogs in here for days and they tried to claw their way out."

"Well, that explains the dog poop," I said.

"Go take down those curtains," mom instructed.

I walked over to the windows and started to pull the curtains down when I saw little white specs that resembled little pellets. I looked a little closer and saw the little white specs were moving.

"Awww!" I screamed.

"What?" my mom asked.

"These things are moving!"

I jumped back and tried to keep from throwing up all over the spaces that we had cleaned already.

"Oh, these are maggots," mom said in a nonchalant way.

"I don't care, I don't want to be here. Can we just go?"

"Lynnie look, once we clean it up, it will be nice. I promise," mom replied.

How can you let me go through this? I thought.

Another Home

We finished and the trailer looked brand new. We got second-hand furniture and I even got a bike once we moved in. I didn't know how, but it was nice, I guessed it was to make up for the dog poop she made me clean. Regardless of the reason, I was happy. I couldn't remember the last time I had received a gift like this. With my new bike in tow, I soon made a friend who lived nearby and we became bike buddies.

One day, my new bike buddy asked to come over.

"Okay, let me check with my mom," I told her.

We rode to my trailer and as soon as we got close, you could hear the commotion from a mile away. Glass was crashing and I could hear my mom screaming.

"Um, let's just go over to your house," I said with embarrassment.

"Okay," she said in a polite manner.

After that, she never asked or spoke about the incident again. My mom had been with Donald for about two years now. It seemed like I would never see my brother again. I missed him and St. Louis in the worse way. And when I thought it couldn't get any worse, it did. Donald brought this woman named Sheila over to the trailer. She had two kids, a boy name Little Donald, who was about two or three and a baby girl named Nicole. I had my own room but Donald gave it to Sheila and her kids. Now I had to sleep on the couch with Bran. Although I was young, I knew this was a hot mess. I used to lay up at night, staring at the now cleaned clawed up walls. Thinking of ways to escape. Where would I go? I didn't want to go to my dad's. I didn't want to go to my Aunts. I was stuck and out of luck.

I found myself thinking of sex all the time. I would think about me and different celebrities. It was funny though because it was me but it wasn't me, I was in someone else's body. I never saw my face, but I had an adult body. Yeah, it was weird.

"Lynnie, we'll be back," my mom said. "Watch the kids."

Now, not only was I watching my bad two-year-old sister, but now I had to watch Shelia's bad kids too. I sat on the couch listening to Nicole cry. Bran was trying to talk to Little Donald, but all he kept doing was making these noises. I didn't notice it at first but Little Donald couldn't say words at all.

At least Bran was saying, "Ba, Ba" when she wanted her bottle and, "Gimme" when she wanted something, but he was older and just making weird screeching noises.

When my mom came back, I asked her about Little Donald.

She just said, "Mind your business."

Oh, okay, see if I watch them again, I thought, because I wouldn't dare say it aloud. It became normal to have these kids with me. I went from taking care of my little sister to being the mother of three kids.

One night out of the blue, my mom told me to get ready. I hopped up and got dress quickly with no questions asked. I got my sister ready. Sheila got her kids ready. It was late, so a lot of things were closed. We pulled up to a strip mall and parked. I wanted to know where we were going, but I didn't ask because I was just happy to be out of the trailer. We all got out of the car.

"Lynnie get the kids."

"Huh?" I said in a frustrated tone.

"All of them?" I whined.

"Yes," she replied.

So, I unbuckled Nicole first, then Brandy and Little Donald last.

"Come on," I said to them.

As I started walking with the kids, I noticed the adults walking in front of us. My mom walked on the right, Donald was in the middle and Sheila was on the left. Sheila was holding Donald around his waist and so was my mom. *WAIT A FREAKING MINUTE!* I thought. I saw my mom moving Sheila's hand off of Donald and vice versa. They were acting like they were my age.

Who's the adult here and why are they fighting over this man, I thought. I was walking with two kids, a baby in a carrier and they were playing *whose man is it anyway!* It was crazy, but normal at the same time normal. The drive back home was nothing but yelling, cursing and name calling. We finally got back to the trailer and a fight broke out. All I could remember was putting the kids in the bedroom and finding Sheila on top of my mom banging her head to the floor. I looked around and connected eyes with my little sister who motioned to the brown wicker chair with the round pillow. For some reason, I knew what she was saying without words. I looked under the pillow and there stood a big butcher knife. I grabbed it and without thought ran to Sheila with the knife up above my head ready to plunge down. All of a sudden, I felt someone's hands grab my hands. It was Donald. When he grabbed me, he flipped me over the coffee table and I ended up hitting my head. He pulled Sheila off of my mom and took her out of the trailer.

"Here take your F******* kids with you, you bastard!" my mom said before going into her room and slamming the door.

She must have cried that entire night. I took Bran into the bedroom with me, but not before I gave her the biggest kiss and hug.

"How did you know?" I asked in a puzzled voice.

Bran just looked at me with her big brown eyes, as if she was saying, "I want him dead too."

I don't know, maybe she wasn't thinking that, but it sure looked like it and her actions that followed would prove me right. Donald came home the next day. My mom really didn't say a word to him or him to her. I don't even think we ate, I mean I fixed Bran some milk but that was it. Later that night, Donald was laying on the couch. I just so happen to come out of my room to find my sister with two forks walking slowly over to Donald. The look in her eyes said it all. She was two years old and walking like a professional hit toddler. I ran over to her, grabbed her and ran into the room. Donald never knew his demise was near.

My mom finally came out of her room and called me in the living room.

"Lynnie, come in here."

I walked into the living room scared, thinking Donald was probably faking sleep and knew the whole time what had happened.

"Lynnie, I want you to pack your things, now." My mom didn't have to tell me twice, I knew exactly what pack your things meant.

"Ernie, where do you think you're going?" Donald asked.

I paused because if he tried to stop up us, I would kill him for sure. Shoot, I'm a minor. My young mind figured I wouldn't get too much time in jail or maybe none at all.

"I'm leaving you bastard, I don't have to be here. I'm going back with my sister."

I stopped in my tracks...Whoa, wait, back it up.

Not Aunt Sherrie's house, I thought.

"Okay," I began talking to myself.

"Lynnie, you have a choice between starving, fighting and possibly going to jail, or you can take your chances with Darius."

Shoot, I decided to take my chances with Darius for a hundred Alex, at least I would be able to eat.

The Effects of Being Me

I became confused. Why did we have to live like this? I thought. I began to feel like this was all that life was, a series of disappointments, hurts, abuse and disgusting living conditions. Moving from place to place made me feel like I didn't belong anywhere. I felt exposed and without any options. I learned to never get my hopes up. I didn't understand why my mother was following behind this man and allowing him to treat her like dirt. Was there a shortage of men? Would this be my life too? Would I belittle myself for the affection of a man?

My standard of life continued to fall, and I didn't think we could sink any lower. It was demeaning to have to clean dog poop and maggots from the place we were going to call home, but I had seen worse. I didn't want to be there. I really wanted to be with my dad, but I thought he didn't want me. That made me feel like something was wrong with me, so my self-esteem continued to suffer.

How could a mother choose drugs over her own kids? How could she go days without feeding us?

The constant fighting, cursing, and name calling that went on embarrassed me and I didn't want anyone to see how I was living. My responsibilities were overwhelming, but I got used to it. I was a kid raising a kid because my mother wasn't even raising us. My sister might as well had been my daughter because I cared for her more than my mother, and I was raising myself, anyway.

I was having thoughts of sex, but I didn't know why. My early sexual experience was marred by frightening episodes of abuse and I was ashamed. Now I found myself thinking about sex and envisioning me having it with others, but I felt like it was me in someone else's body.

Would my experiences leave me unable to achieve appropriate relationships involving trust, closeness and positive sexual expression? Was sex all I was good for? I harbored these feelings inside and my self-worth suffered.

My mind was so gone that I almost killed Sheila. How could I even think about killing someone? I wasn't a killer, was I? I had so much anger and hostility that I just wanted all the madness to end. I'm glad I realized that was not the way.

Letter to My Younger Self

Lynnie,

First of all, I'm so glad you didn't kill Donald or Sheila even though I know at times you felt like they were ruining your life. In reality, the experiences were making you stronger.

The funny thing about life, we all think nothing bad can happen to us. It's easy to think that bad things happen to other people. When you see someone go through something so horrible and mind blowing, you feel bad but are secretly grateful you aren't them. Now you understand what it feels like to be *them*.

Understand, bad things happen to good people and you my dear are definitely a good person. To get through this situation, you must be strong and resilient. You must know that you are not your situation and have no control over the decisions your mother made that got you there and you must release that burden.

The drugs had a hold of mom and she was lost. It wasn't you that was driving her to drugs, it was the weight of the world. It's a good thing you have strong shoulders. The physical hunger that you felt will later fuel the spiritual hunger that God has placed inside you. Your responsibility did force you to grow up fast, but it was preparing you.

I know the constant fighting, cursing, and name calling embarrassed you, but you can't control what others do, you can only control your actions. Vow that you will break the cycle and be better. You are not your circumstances, so don't feel this is a permanent situation. This too shall pass.

The thoughts of sex you're having are your way of coping with the trauma you suffered. Your early sexual experience was marred by frightening episodes of abuse and you were ashamed, which is normal. You've had wrong things done to you, but there is nothing wrong with you.

One day you will be able to have an appropriate relationship involving trust, closeness and positive sexual expression. Remember, there is so much good inside of you. It's your job to uncover it. You are valuable beyond measure. Lynnie, the madness will end one day, but until then be strong and courageous. The victory will be yours.

Sincerely,

Lynn

Your Future Self

This Can't Be Life Commentary

Matthew 10:29-31 Are not two sparrows sold for a farthing? And one of them shall not fall on the ground without your Father. But the very hairs of your head are all numbered. Fear ye not therefore, ye are of more value than many sparrows.

God's creatures are under the protection of His word, insomuch that nothing befalls them without His direction; and therefore, your enemies cannot touch even your bodies without your heavenly Father's permission. But he will also watch your hand and protect you from doing something that could harm yourself. He will watch over you.

Reflections For Your Journey

- Don't allow the challenges of life make you bitter, realize there is a sweet part that you will get to.

- Don't be ashamed by the actions of another that you cannot control.

- Allow yourself to explore your thoughts and know it's ok to have them, your mind is just trying to figure the world out.

- Don't settle, you are royalty and deserve to be treated as such.

- Know that what you are going through is temporary and it will pass, but you have to hold on.

- You can choose happiness whenever you wish no matter what your circumstances are.

- You deserve to be loved.

Beyond What You See

Journal

Lynn Barnes

Chapter Eight
On High Alert

"A heart well prepared for adversity in bad times hopes, and in good times fears for a change in fortune."
~Horace

We moved back with my Aunt Sherrie and I was on high alert all the time. If Darius was home, I would leave and go outside. I kept my distance even from him. My aunt had a friend that stayed down the street named Bobbie Joe. Bobbie was a six feet ten, high yellow biker with long curly black hair. He stayed in this big green house on the corner. My mom liked him and he liked her. I liked it there because it was spacious and it was his. He was a gentle giant, but intimidating nonetheless. He had a friend named Sam who would come over often to visit. Sam reminded me of Grady from the Sanford & Son television show in the seventies. He looked like he hadn't shaved in weeks and had a few scars on his face; definitely not someone you wanted to run into in a dark alley.

Every time he came to visit Bobbie Joe, I watched him like a hawk because he was intimidating and I didn't know what he was capable of. During one of his visits, I was sitting there observing his every move when I saw him slowly slide his hand into his pocket. I knew he was about to pull out a gun or a knife and stab us all, but to my surprise he was armed with a yellow box of Lemon Head candies. He pulled them out and popped them in his mouth with a slight cringe as the sour taste hit his taste buds. It was one of the funniest things I had seen, but I guess it also showed me not to judge a book by its cover.

Although I still believed Sam could inflict pain, this day, the only thing he was smashing was sweets. Bobbie Joe took us a lot of places. One day my mom asked him to take us to the carnival. He never had a problem saying yes to my mom. Going to the carnival was one of the best days of my life; I enjoyed it so much. All I kept thinking to myself was, *I'm free!*

The Best Day Ever

That day I was free from all the drama, the stealing, the fighting, the molestation and all the pain I felt. I was happy even if the feeling would not last, because it never did, I just enjoyed the moment. I couldn't remember having more fun. I played all the midway games to win prizes. I rode roller coasters, the Ferris wheel and all the rides that spun around faster than anything I had seen and ate more cotton candy than I should have.

As night time grew near, the lights from the carnival, smell of buttered popcorn, sounds of people laughing and screams of excitement intoxicated me. Freedom came over me for the first time in a long time. I could relax and be twelve years old. No taking care of Bran, no making sure we had what we needed, no wondering if my mom was ok. That day, I enjoyed the moment because I wanted to replace the ones that were giving me nightmares.

The carnival was closing, and as we walked back to Bobbie Joe's camper, I had the biggest smile on my face. I even walked with a little pep. Bran and I got inside, but my mom and Bobbie Joe stood outside the door. I sat there and looked around the camper. I pretended it was ours and Bobbie Joe was my dad. The things I noticed were a big bag of marijuana, some half-smoked joints and a gun with several bullets laying beside it. I had been around enough drugs in my life to recognize most, so I knew what it was.

My thought was that weed was not crack, so it wasn't as bad. I justified the gun because I felt we would need something to protect us if Donald showed his face again. I slid over to the middle seat of the camper to get a good look at my mom and Bobbie Joe who were both outside. Suddenly, he jerked over and over again and then he fell.

"Bobbie, Bobbie!" my mom screamed as she shook him.

"Bobbie, oh my God!" she screamed as she jumped in the camper.

"I need to call the ambulance. I'll be right back ok."

"Okay," I said calmly.

She ran down the road to the pay phone. As I sat there and waited, I looked over at my sleeping sister and thought, Oh my God, I have to hide this stuff!

I figured if the ambulance was coming, so were the cops. I grabbed Bobbie Joe's stuff that would have landed him in jail and looked around for somewhere to hide it all. I remembered seeing Bobbie use a secret compartment under one bench in the trailer. I put everything in there and sat on it. My mom soon returned. She checked on Bobbie then jumped in the camper in a panic.

I noticed that she was looking around for something.

"Where is it... where is it?" she said.

I got up and opened the top part of the bench to reveal the stash. My mom looked at me with tears in her eyes. She grabbed me around my neck and hugged me. I guess she was hurt because I had to do it, but glad I knew enough to hide the contraband.

"Put it back down and sit back," she instructed me.

I did just that. The ambulance came and my mom went outside with them. Sure enough, the police were right behind them. While the paramedics worked on Bobbie Joe, one of the police officers opened the door and climb into the camper.

"Hi, how are you?" he asked me.

"I'm okay."

"How old are you?"

"Twelve."

"Did you see what happened?"

"Yes."

"Can you tell me?"

"Yes."

"Okay," the officer replied.

So, I told him what happened, how we went to the carnival and how Bobbie Joe jerked and fell.

"Is that all that happened?"

"Yes."

"Okay, thank you."

My mom was standing outside the open door. When the police officer walked out, she walked in, sat down beside me and held me.

The police officer came back to the door and said, "They will take him to the hospital, can you drive?"

My mom answered, "Yes."

Mom hopped in the driver's seat and followed the ambulance to the hospital. Bobbie Joe survived but he wouldn't remain in our lives for long. We stayed in California for a few months after that, and within that period a reoccurring nightmare of Donald coming back into the picture resurfaced and we went back to moving from house to house.

The Effects of Being Me

I stayed on high alert. I was never comfortable because I knew if I was, my guard would fall and I would subject myself to being molested again. All the while I was tightly wired, like a spring, never able to relax, always on alert. My childhood wasn't normal, and I don't mean that in a quirky way. I was a victim of incest and abuse. What happened to me was done by my uncle and my cousin.

None of what I heard, read or had been told gave me a definition for what was happening. In my mind abuse wasn't your favorite uncle or cousin climbing on top of you or touching you in places you were yet to even explore until you froze up and zoned out and let it happen. I never repressed the memories of my experiences or horrifying details. The memory of who I thought I was would come into my mind and destroy any feelings of normalcy. I couldn't be anything good doing these things.

Even though I guarded my secret with my life, I wanted to be found out. I couldn't imagine telling anyone though. What would I say? I was a child who knew little about traditional sex, let alone its taboo variations.

I admired my cousin, but he was destroying me. It wasn't just physically; it was mentally, but I still admired and looked up to Darius. What on earth do you do in a situation like that when you're a kid? If everyone around me knew, then I wouldn't be able to pretend it hadn't happened. Pretending the abuse wasn't real was the only thing that made my life bearable.

I was so thirsty for a father figure I imagined Bobbie Joe was my dad. I had a certain freedom when I was around him. I was in self-induced bondage for so long. In need of that male role model to help mold me, love me and show me how to be loved. I needed him to tell me I was beautiful and that everything would be ok. I came to enjoy each moment we had with Bobbie Joe because I didn't know how long they would last. All the good things in my life seemed to be temporary, but the pain was continuous.

I was happy that I didn't need to steal anymore. Just by shopping with my mom I was unaware I had committed more crimes before the age of twelve than most juvenile offenders by default. I was surrounded by dysfunction and learned how to navigate it. That same dysfunction gave me the instinct to hide the contraband in Bobbie Joe's trailer. I wanted nothing to happen to him; he was my dad in my head and I needed him to stay, but most good things in my life were short lived and would soon disappear.

I could tell how my mother looked at me, that I made her happy and sad at the same time. Probably because I reminded her of who she used to be, which reminded her of how far she had fallen. I guess she wanted more for my life. This wasn't what my mother intended for either of us.

Letter to My Younger Self

Lynnie,

Let me first say, sexual abuse is the ultimate trauma. You have gone through something very traumatic, but you will get through it even though it doesn't feel like it now. The guilt, shame and blame you might feel because you could not stop the abuse must be released. It is important for you to understand that it was the person who hurt you that should be held accountable—not you.

As an adult, intimacy might be a struggle. You may experience flashbacks or painful memories while engaging in sexual activity, even though it is consensual and on your own terms. You may also struggle to set boundaries that help you feel safe in relationships, but know you must work towards that goal when the time comes.

You may struggle with low self-esteem, which may result from you being violated or ignored. But know this too shall pass and your pain is giving you strength to walk in your purpose.

Share your secret with someone you trust. Let them know you have been violated and need help, this action can save you years of hurt and pain. One day you will forgive Darius, because he doesn't know the extent of what he is doing to hurt you. Pretending it didn't happen is the wrong thing to do. You must face it head on and know in your weakness God makes you strong.

Sexual abuse does not mandate you will live a tragic, pain-filled life forever. Yet there are cases in which victims of sexual abuse learn to explore the experience of abuse and, in doing so, transform their identities from victim to survivor. The goal is to work at increasing your self-esteem and knowing who God created you to be. You have control over your life allow no one to take that away from you.

Don't allow the sadness and fear to paralyze you. You are a survivor which separates those who haven't successfully coped and those who have. Examine your feelings, rather than acting them out in future relationships.

Write in a journal and express your thoughts so you don't keep them bottled up inside. Sharing your thoughts and feelings about the abuse is incredibly helpful. The goal is to get your feelings out, regardless if you are writing, typing or talking them out.

Find a place in your mind that feels safe and restorative to develop a coping mechanism. This will do wonders for your soul. As you're striving for balance, find activities that make you happy and remember that your mental wellbeing is important too.

Don't focus on what is wrong but identify what's right. You have the strength, empowerment, courage and perseverance to overcome any obstacle. Think about it... you've been raising a baby since you were ten.

Sincerely,

Lynn

Your Future Self

On High Alert Commentary

Matt 10:28 NLT Don't be afraid of those who want to kill your body; they cannot touch your soul. Fear only God, who can destroy both soul and body in hell.

People have no power to injure the soul, the immortal part of you. The body is a small matter in comparison to the soul. Temporal death is a slight thing compared with eternal death. He directs us, not to be alarmed at the prospect of temporal death, but to fear God, who can destroy both soul and body forever. This passage proves that the bodies of the wicked will be raised up to be punished forever. Just because I was molested, they could not kill what God had placed inside of me.

Reflections For Your Journey

✦ What happened? Write down everything you can remember.

✦ Why do you think this happened to you?

✦ Who do you blame for what happened and why?

✦ How do you feel toward the other people involved?

✦ How did this event affect how you feel about yourself?

✦ How did it affect your relationships in the past and today?

✦ What triggers these memories for you?

Beyond What You See

Journal

Lynn Barnes

Chapter Nine
Little Mother

"The price of greatness is responsibility."
~Winston Churchill

We rode on the Amtrak train going back to St. Louis. I remember sitting looking out the window with tears coming down my face. I was happy to finally go back. As my mind wandered I thought back to the earlier years back in St. Louis, prior to the robbery.

My cousin D.D was having a sleepover, and I asked my mom if I could go.

She said, "Yes, but you have to take your sister."

"What?" I exclaimed.

My sister was a baby, and I had to take her with me to my very first sleepover. She cried nonstop, and I was so embarrassed. I eventually decided it was best if I left, but after getting in the car Bran stopped crying and I was able to go back. At that moment, I knew things would be different. Now I had responsibilities.

Watching Bran was something we did on a regular basis by this point. Usually, everything went fine because my brother and I were pretty responsible even at a young age. One day, Twan and I were watching Bran. We watched TV while she slept in our room, but I guess we didn't hear her wake up. Eventually, we heard a sound. She wasn't crying like she normally did, it was more like gurgling and cooing. I walked into our room to get her and saw that she had gotten the Vaseline and it wasn't pretty. As I stood there, my life flashed before my eyes. Bran had smeared it all over the floor, her hair, clothes, and face. It was everywhere.

"Twan!" I screamed.

He ran in the room.

"Oh my God, get a towel quick. If momma sees this, we're dead," Twan said.

I ran to get the towel, and we started wiping away. It was messy and very hard to get up. It just kept smearing worse.

"I don't want to get the cord," I said as tears ran down my face.

"Go wet it, I'll start cleaning Bran."

So, I rushed to wet the towel and wiped and wiped until it was clean. Twan wiped the Vaseline off of Brandy's face and changed her clothes. I tried wiping it out of her hair but it wouldn't come out, so I took her barrettes down and redid her hair.

Yes, it was very shiny, but my excuse would have been, *Momma, I just wanted to fix her hair for you.*

Everything was clean, and we looked at each other, smiled and gave each other high fives for the teamwork. Soon, we heard the keys at the front door.

"Hey," my mom said.

"Hey mom," we said in unison. She quickly grabbed for Brandy.

"Come here boo,"

As she took Bran in her arms, Twan and I went into the living room to enjoy the butt wippin' free moment.

"Antwan and Lynn, bring your a**** here!"

We looked at each other; I began crying immediately. *What did we miss?* I thought.

"But we cleaned it all up Twan," I said.

We walked into the room.

"Why in the hell is she pissy wet?"

"Go get the cord, now!"

There were so many times I can recall being beat due to mom not approving of my mothering style or for mistakes I made while watching my baby sister. I know it sounds crazy, but that was my reality. By the time my sister Bran was three-years-old, I did it all. I fed her, I washed her up and I put her to bed. For all intents and purposes, I was her mother.

Not only was I a mother to Bran, but I still had to obey my mother's commands. She always had me make her coffee and I hated it. One night, she asked me to make her coffee and I was so tired of doing stuff for everybody else. I went into the kitchen, put water into the pot and put it on the stove. After getting out the coffee, creamer, and sugar the water began boiling.

As I was taking it off of the stove, Brandy was pulling on me saying, "Gimme, gimme."

"You want some?" I asked as I was bending over towards her.

As I was saying it, I had the pot of boiling hot water in my hands. I didn't realize I was tipping the pot as I was bending and the water began pouring out of the pot and splashing down on her face, neck, and arm. The scream I heard killed me. I heard ringing in my ears and I blacked out. The sound of my mom cursing and screaming snapped me out of it. I saw my mom going for a stack of two by fours piled in the corner of the kitchen. I didn't speak a word. I jetted out the door, and if you know about California weather, you know it gets up in the hundreds during the day and the sixties at night. I was barefoot, only wearing shorts and a short sleeve shirt. I walked and walked, never looking back. *This is it, I'm leaving, I'm on my own now*, I thought.

Tears rushed down my face. I was freezing but didn't care. I told myself that I was never returning. The next thing I knew, the big blue van was driving slowly beside me and I was scared. I didn't want to get beat; I didn't want to deal with this anymore. I would have rather died out there on the streets than get back in that van. The side door opened.

"Come here, baby," my mom said in a soft nurturing tone.

I stood there and didn't move. *You're not tricking me*, I thought.

"Come here Lynnie."

I crept over to the open door. My mom got out and hugged me.

"Get in."

It was so suspect. I knew they were getting ready to knock me off and drop my body somewhere in the woods. I opened the door and walked to the back and sat down on the cold steel floor of Donald's gutted blue van that only had a passenger seat and driver seat. I wrapped my arms around my cold legs and rested my head on my knees. Bran came to the back to sit with me. She rubbed my face and everything felt ok with the world.

I held her and said, "I'm sorry, I didn't mean to hurt you."

She kept rubbing my face. I noticed my mom looking back at us and smiling. I still felt like it was suspect and everyone was in on it. It wasn't long before we were kicked out of that house and began living in that van.

Some days were harder than others, but what I hated most was when Donald would drive to a park and they would make Bran and I play outside while they would get high in the van. We would take a wash up in the park bathroom before or after we played.

I can remember the scorching hot days with no relief, not even in the shade. Many days, I would pray for night time to come. It was too hot to cope. I was done, this was my life but it felt like my hell and I made the choice to accept it.

Donald was slick; you had to watch him closely. He did slick things to benefit himself but made it seem like he was helping you. I remember him attempting to teach me how to fight in case I ever needed to. He jerked me by my hair a few times and stepped on my foot. He also showed me his penis. *Now how will this help me to fight?* I thought.

"It's important for you to know what one of these looks like," he said.

Then he made me touch it. I hated him even more. He made me sick to my stomach. I told my mom, even though I knew in my heart she still wouldn't leave him, but I didn't care. I had to tell this time. I couldn't keep this to myself.

In a small way, I was hoping she would have a, "You can do whatever you want to me, but don't touch my daughter!" rant I had seen on TV, but that did not happen.

The Effects of Being Me

Guilt is a valuable emotion because it helps to maintain your ties to people. I felt responsible for my little sister so the mistake hurt me when I hurt her. I held myself responsible for everyone. So, when I could not protect my sister because I wasn't paying attention to what I was doing I felt terrible. The feelings were overwhelming. I felt terrible because of the unrealistic expectations I put on myself to be a little mother to my sister. I felt an internal sense of pressure and guilt.

Homelessness influenced every area of my life. The lack of secure shelter stifled my development. I was confronted with stressful and traumatic events that I was too young to understand, therefore leading to emotional distress. The constant change of moving and the insecurities of not knowing where I would sleep each night was wearing on me and would soon manifest in my behavior.

I felt like my development was delayed and my sense of security was shattered. My emotions were a wreck, my foundation was shaken and I needed support but did not understand where to find it. Although I was with my mother and Donald, I was alone and on my own. If I made a mistake it wasn't just me who suffered, it was my little sister Bran too. My mother made mistakes daily and didn't seem to think about the consequences.

I dreaded when people at school asked me where I lived or if we could hang out at my place. I would try to give my schoolmates a general response, maybe the name of a neighborhood, but they always pressed for more. I didn't want to tell them I didn't have a home. It was embarrassing to say I had been homeless on and off for most of my adolescent years.

Living in the van meant Bran and I had to get out and play while mom and Donald did their drugs. I often felt like the drugs were more important than we were. Perhaps other students in my school lived like I did, but I never knew it, so it made me feel like I was the only one suffering like I was.

Letter to My Younger Self

Lynnie,

Although you've suffered many disappointments, know there is more to life and you will discover it if you stay resilient. You have been exposed to more than most people your age will ever see and it was building you rather than destroying you. Although you felt like your options were minimal God was making a way for you out of your mess.

Although your mother is lost, she loves you, but has become a slave to a substance that is controlling her. Your real mother is buried deep inside fighting to escape. The drugs are making decisions for her.

Mom's capacity to deal with her reality has diminished. She's fallen victim to whatever could make her feel numb, not realizing she is zoning out right through your childhood leaving you to fin for yourself.

She chose drugs as her escape and you have became collateral damage. Her actions are not a reflection of who you are, but rather what she is dealing with.

Don't allow her choices to dictate how you live your life going forward. God needs you to be responsible, so He allowed some of the things to happen in order to prepare you for a fallen world. You were sent to be the change that needed to take place. You are a cycle breaker with determination to break the cycle of abuse, rape, drugs, and molestation.

Don't be ashamed that you are living in a van. This is your lot in life, meaning where God has you, but He will elevate you. You must learn all you can where you are and watch Him move on your behalf. The Lord provides manna for the day; therefore He will supply all of your needs.

Sincerely,

Lynn
Your Future Self

Little Mother Commentary

Psalm 34:17-20 ESV - When the righteous cry for help, the Lord hears and delivers them out of all their troubles. The Lord is near to the brokenhearted and saves the crushed in spirit. Many are the afflictions of the righteous, but the Lord delivers him out of them all. He keeps all his bones; not one of them is broken.

Learn to fear the Lord, if you desire true comfort here on earth, and eternal happiness in Heaven. Those who serve God are the happiest. We must look further than the present world to find our happiness. Man's life on earth consist of only a few days and many of those are full of trouble, but see the good in all things and guard your heart by watching what you allow in. Guard your tongue by monitoring the words you speak. Learn to be useful…to live God's purpose. Seek peace, pursue it and be willing to deny ourselves. It is the constant practice of true believers when in distress, to cry unto God. Be humble and seek righteousness and it is their constant comfort He hears them. It's necessary to have a contrite heart. When this is accomplished every grace will flourish, and nothing can encourage such a one but the free, rich grace of the gospel of Jesus Christ. He will protect you. Whatever troubles you encounter, shall not hurt your soul, for God keeps you from sinning in troubles.

Reflections For Your Journey

- I accept my responsibility for nurturing those gifted to me.

- My ability to conquer my challenges is limitless.

- I am courageous and I stand up for myself.

- Everything that is happening now is happening for my ultimate good.

- My fears of tomorrow are simply melting away.

Beyond What You See

Journal

Lynn Barnes

Chapter Ten
Feeling Like A Freed Slave

"Slavery is hell. Freedom is heaven. Deception is warfare. Honesty is peace."
~Joshua Aaron Guillory

We finally arrived back in St. Louis. My mind had been filled with memories during the trip, now I had to face the present. Even though I felt my dad didn't want me, I wanted him. I had not realized the extent of how much I needed him to be what a father is supposed to be in a young girl's life. Although I wanted him in my life more than anything, I don't know if it would have hurt me more to be rejected yet again. But I was willing to risk my feelings being hurt for a chance to have him in my life.

The path I was on was not what I wanted for my life. At this point, I was fourteen, but I felt like I was in my twenties. I was tired and worn out. I was five-foot-ten, about a hundred and twenty pounds. My hair was a puffy dried up curl, I was a mess. The last year we were in California, my Aunt Sherrie and my two cousins had already moved back to St. Louis, I guess that's why my mom decided to move. I didn't know for sure and frankly, I didn't care.

Once we got to St. Louis, we went right over to my grams house, but I was eager to get to my dad's. My dad showed up at my grams house later that day. I ran into his arms hoping this wasn't a one-time visit. I held him tight, praying that he would feel the fear that I had throughout my body.

The pain of separation and my desire to have my dad in my life was overwhelming. I had come out of a war and was suffering from post-traumatic stress. I felt like I had a chance to escape my hell to live the life I dreamed about.

"Hey Sweetie," dad said. I just looked at him. Please don't let that be the sweetie I think it is.

"Hey, daddy!"

"When are we going to your house?"

"Where is Antwan?"

"He's at the house, where is your mom?"

"She's in the kitchen."

He rubbed my hair, and then walked into the kitchen. I walked in behind him. If he's going to cop out again, I wanted to hear him say it.

"Hey everybody!"

Everyone spoke back.

"Can I talk to you?" dad said looking my mom's way.

They walked into the dining room. I tried eavesdropping but my grams kept asking me questions.

"Come here, Lynnette."

I walked over to her.

"Ma'am."

"What you want to eat?"

"It doesn't matter," I replied.

I was trying to get back to the eavesdropping. My dad comes into the kitchen.

"You ready," he asked.

Hallelujah! I thought.

"Yes, let me get my things." I responded.

I ran upstairs so fast, praying that he was still downstairs when I got back.

"I got em!"

I didn't say goodbye to my mom, my grams, no one; I ran straight out of the house to the bat mobile, the name Twan and I had given dad's car. When I turned around, I saw my mom holding Bran, walking towards the car. *What is she doing? I hope she's not coming*, I thought. I slowly moved from the front passenger door to the back. We all got in the car. I didn't know what to think. *Is she staying with us too?* I wondered.

"Ma, why are you going?"

"What, you don't want me to go?"

No, I said to myself.

"I want to see my son."

"Oh," I replied.

I hoped that was all she wanted to do. I didn't want her living with us. I couldn't bare the thought of leaving again. It didn't matter what my dad did or didn't do, all I knew is when I was with him, we ate, we had clothes (not maternity clothes) and we had a roof over our heads at all times. I was not going back and I was ready to run away before I did. The more I thought about it, my life had become my own personal prison, and I was determined to escape.

We pulled up to a high rise off Grand. It was near Laclede town where we use to stay. We got out the car and I looked around the area to survey my surroundings. I was so happy to be here. I was anxious about seeing my brother. I remembered the deep voice on the phone and wondered if he had a mustache too. My excitement grew as we got to the door of the apartment. My heart started pounding so hard. My dad couldn't get the door open quick enough. Once inside, I saw my brother come around the corner.

"Twan!"

"Hey, sis!"

We hugged and I remember never wanting to let him go.

"Hey sis, how are you?"

"I'm okay now."

"Hey baby," my mom chimed in.

"Hey, ma."

They hugged and my dad started dinner.

"You need any help?" my mom asked. I turned and looked at her. *Oh, now you want to cook?* I thought. It's not that my mom didn't cook, it's just when she got with Donald, cooking seemed like a distant memory.

Twan walked me to his room.

"You'll be sleeping in here."

"But isn't this your room?"

"I'll sleep on the couch," Twan said.

"Twan, I don't want to take your room."

"Sis, it's ok."

I put my things in his bedroom and sat on the bed. I wanted to cry. This must have been what a freed slave felt like. Dinner was ready, and we all sat down to eat. I looked around the table and smiled inside.

My mom stayed over that night, but I didn't care. The next day, my dad took my mom back to my grandmother's house without me. I couldn't believe it, I was actually staying. The emotions I felt in that moment gave me a sense of peace that my body hadn't felt in a very long time. Over the next couple of months, I traveled back and forth from my dad's to my grams. My dad worked a lot, so he didn't want me to be at home alone.

My brother was in ROTC and did things after school sometimes. I enjoyed going over my grams. My cousin Kayla was there, and she made it fun. Kayla was different. She always dressed better than I did anyway, but she seemed more mature and sophisticated. While I was a tall, lanky, tom boyish looking girl with a dry Jeri Curl fro, Kayla was the one who brought my femininity out.

Kayla put a relaxer in my hair and styled it. For the first time in a long time, I felt pretty. Kayla took me under her wing just like in California. I envied her. She was always so beautiful, smart, funny and everyone always gravitated towards her. I wanted that.

Kayla had a boyfriend named Marlon. He was short, but taller than Kayla. He was dark chocolate and bowlegged. He also had other brothers, one named Alan. Although I didn't have a type, Alan wasn't it. He was too short for me.

One day, we went over to Marlon's house and there he was, this tall fair skinned guy with a short shag Jeri Curl. His name was Matthew Johnson. He looked older because he had a mustache.

"Hi," Mathew said.

I paused for a moment, and then looked around. He couldn't have been talking to me. I was a nobody.

"I'm talking to you," he said with a smile.

"Oh, hi," I said with an even bigger smile. I was cheesing from ear to ear, like the *Kool-Aid Man*.

"So, your Kayla's cousin."

"Yes," I replied.

"How old are you?"

"Fourteen, but I'll be Fifteen in July."

"How old are you?"

"Sixteen."

Yes, I thought with excitement.

"So, you're here from California?" Matthew asked.

He already knew a lot of information about me, I thought.

"Um, yes," I said.

"Are you going back?"

"Dang, I just got back, are you ready for me to leave already?"

We both laughed and we hit it off from there. My birthday was approaching, but I wasn't getting excited about it, because I hadn't celebrated it in a while. The only thing that excited me was going over to my grams to see Matthew. He was very intriguing. He would wear plaid shirts and shorts to match with a pair of loafers and no socks. It seemed like he had every color of this outfit and he would keep a toothbrush in his mouth to match his outfit. Yes, it was weird, but it was St. Louis in the eighties. It was a sexy weird. He had pretty teeth, so I could see the deal with the toothbrush. Matthew was welcomed at my gram's house. He came over every time I visited. I was falling for him fast.

There were boys I liked back then, but I dated no one. I'm sure if I had a boyfriend while I lived with my mom, she would not have cared. I don't know, I guess I wasn't thinking about it, but I was now. My mind was free enough to not be consumed with simply surviving.

As we sat on the couch in my grams living room, Matthew scooted closer.

"What are you doing for your birthday?" Matthew asked.

"I don't know, my dad may do something, but I'm not sure."

"I want to come back over."

"What!" I replied.

"Come back over!"

"What do you mean, come back over?"

"You can't come back over here."

"Why not?" Matthew asked.

"Um, because," I replied.

"Because what?"

This fool was persistent.

"I'll see."

"I hope you do because I want to give you your birthday present," Matthew said.

He leaned over and kissed me.

"Okay," I said.

I would have given anything to see the goofy smile on my face. I walked Matthew to the door and at that moment, I knew I would sneak him in the house. I went downstairs in the basement to talk with Kayla.

"I need your help."

"My help with what?" Kayla asked.

"Matthew wants to come back over later," I replied.

"Later!"

"What, what do you me mean later?"

"Like later, later," I said.

"Oh no."

"I didn't know he liked you like that."

"Huh," I replied.

"I mean, I know he likes you but he was just supposed to hang out with you, so you wouldn't feel left out. Now he wants to sneak in the house?"

Okay, so Matthew was just being nice so I wouldn't be the third wheel? Oh really! So I decided to tell him no to the idea of coming back over. I ran the conversation in my head several times before he called. When the moment arrived, I was stern in my tone and brief, "Look Matthew, I can't let you back in, there's just no way."

He responded in a soft smooth tone, "Look Lynnette, if you don't want me to come over, just say so, but I think I'm falling in love with you."

Okay, first off, he called me Lynnette and no one calls me that but my grams. I haven't heard a guy talk like that before or say my name that way. His smooth voice was persuasive and made me relax. It made me feel wanted, needed and loved. I wanted more of that.

"Look Matthew, I didn't say you couldn't come over, I was saying you couldn't come over until everyone was asleep."

That night, I snuck him in and he made me feel beautiful from the inside out. Matthew made me forget all the bad that happened in the past. I was happy and in love. I thought about Matthew constantly. I couldn't get enough of him. My grams loved him and when my mom was there, she loved him too. My dad knew nothing about him. I would sneak him in after my dad went to sleep and sneak him out before my dad came home. When my dad did find out about him, it was from a phone call Matthew's aunt made to my dad to tell him how she caught us in her home. I was a crazed teenager. I put every ounce of feelings I had into him. My dad didn't care about those feelings. He chewed me out.

He called me all kinds of names and said, "Don't end up like your mother!"

The ride after that was quiet. I didn't speak to him and he didn't speak to me. I didn't care what my father said, I didn't want to be like my mom, but I was not leaving Matthew.

One day, I was over my grams house and her friend Jackie was there with her niece Kim. Kim was much older, tall, and light skinned with long beautiful hair. I thought nothing of it. I spoke and waited for Matthew to come over. There was a knock at the door. It was Matthew, so I let him in. While we were talking, his eyes bypassed my face. I turned around to see what he was looking at, and there she was just standing there.

"Who is she?" Matthew asked.

"Oh, this is Kim my grandma's friend's niece."

They shook hands and they both had this gaze thing going on. I thought, did I just hook these two up? Maybe I was overreacting. A few days later I came to visit my grams and there Matthew was sitting on the couch.

"What are you doing here?" I asked.

"Oh, I was waiting for you."

"But you didn't know I was coming over."

"I figure you would be," Matthew replied.

So, being young and dumb, I thought nothing about it, until Kim walked through the front door. She was going through some things, so Jackie asked my grams if she could stay there for a while.

"Hey," she said looking at Matthew.

"Hey Kim, what are you doing here?" I said with confusion.

"I'm staying with Mrs. Gladys for a while," Kim said.

I looked at her then looked at him.

"Can I talk to you for a minute, outside?"

We walked out the front door on to the porch.

"Is there something I need to know?"

"No, what are you talking about?" Matthew asked.

"Matthew, you didn't know I was coming over, and I didn't know Kim stayed here now."

"Look Lynnette, I want to be with you, I do, but I like her."

I'm sorry, but am I getting punk'd right now? *Okay, where are the cameras,* I thought.

"You're playing, right?" I said.

As Matthew was about to answer, Kim poked her head out the door.

"Matthew, can you come here for a moment?"

He looked at me.

"I'm sorry," he said and walked into the house.

Beyond What You See

I stood there, waiting for the joke to end. I waited for at least ten minutes, but no one came back out. I couldn't go back into my grandma's house, I was so embarrassed. I walked down the steps and walked straight to the bus stop and went home. I remember crying for so long. My head was hurting, my eyes where blood shot red and my body hurt. I never knew your body could hurt so badly. It took a while before I could get the nerve to go back over there. When I did, I was hoping not to bump into Matthew. It took some time to get over it, but I eventually did.

I found out that Matthew wasn't sixteen when I met him, he was in fact nineteen. It all made since. I didn't mean anything to him, I couldn't have. But I fell in love with him and it hurt. How could I stop feeling like this? I wanted it to go away, but it didn't.

The Effects of Being Me

Going back to St. Louis made me feel like I was going home. I told myself that I didn't care If my dad didn't want me there. I knew I wanted to be there and it was bothering me. I wanted my dad in my life no matter what. I felt I needed a father figure to protect me. Maybe if dad was here, all of these bad things would have never happened to me.

I was going down the wrong path and I saw it, but didn't know how to correct it. I felt old and worn out. After being molested multiple times, verbally and physically abused, I was a mess. Seeing my dad made me miss him even more. I wanted him to accept and love me. I cried tears of joy when I ran into his arms and hugged him tight. I wanted him to feel the fear I had throughout my body. I felt like if I was in his presence he couldn't brush me off with a *Sweetie*.

Moving with my dad gave me a sense of security again but I had to learn how to live there. What I didn't like was that dad had no pictures of his first family anywhere. We were absent and that's how I felt about him being in my life…absent.

I felt like a freed slave. I was happy to be out of what I believed to be bondage, but living in a new place was like moving to a foreign land.

I was now vulnerable to deception and fake perceptions that I put my trust and all of my emotions into the first boy who showed me attention. When Kayla took me under her wing, I felt beautiful. I didn't have much but she worked with what I had. When Matthew talked to me that first day, I thought he saw in me what I felt. When you're empty for so long and yearning for attention, affection and love you can get caught up and misguided. Matthew took what was left of my heart and broke it. I was fresh off of the slave ship, free from bondage and daily imprisonment. I wasn't mentally ready for that kind of love.

Letter to My Younger Self

Lynnie,

It's great you're moving back to St. Louis and that you feel free, but remember freedom comes with a price. Although you aren't with your mom in California, you have to be conscious of the decisions you make and how you treat this newfound freedom. Your dad wants you but the situation is complex. You are all your mother has and he would be taking you from her. Although he may not have handled the transition right, he's operating within his capacity and doing what he can or knows, based off how he was raised.

Lynnie, know when your earthly father isn't present, your heavenly father is and He will always protect you and guide you. You have to talk with Him regularly through prayer and He will provide. I know you wish your father was there to protect you from all you've experienced, but just know God was there and He will use your pain for His purpose so He can be glorified.

I'm sorry you got your heart broken by Matthew. I know that it feels very different from other hurts you've encounter. Don't let this keep you from letting someone love you like you deserve to be loved. Although he took advantage of your innocence and naive mind, your still strong and will come through this pain.

You must correct your path by finding people that will guide you. That may not be an easy task, but it will change your life for the better. Show people who you are and they will have a desire to help you and mentor you on this journey to freedom. Don't let how you feel dictate your worth. You are beautifully and wonderfully made. You need to rest to rejuvenate your spirit. Read whatever you can get your hands on and fill your mind with possibilities of the life you imagine.

Although they hurt your body and tried to crush your soul, they can't because you are strong in Christ.

Know your father accepts you, loves you and feels your fear. He wishes he could take all of your hurt away but as you know that is a tall order that only our Savior can fulfill. When dad calls you Sweetie, it isn't a brush off but rather a term of endearment he uses when he doesn't know what to do.

Rest in your new security and relish in the moment with your dad. You can't get the years you lost back but don't harbor ill will or negative feelings towards him because he is the only dad you will have and he is doing his best. Although you need more, God will make sure you have it.

God loves you and He will not let any weapon that was created against you prosper.

Sincerely,

Lynn
Your Future Self

Lynn Barnes

Freed Slave Commentary

Galatians 5:1 - It is for freedom that Christ has set us free. Stand firm, then, and do not let yourselves be burdened again by a yoke of slavery.

It is necessary we first see what liberty is. Christ makes His people free. But He cannot free you as long as your own conscience keeps you bound up into the fear of death and punishment. If you are afraid to explore your mind, you can never expand; and the mind which cannot expand, is never free.

To receive this blessing, we must feel God's love and be guided by Him. We must accept the whole will of God, because it is the will of the one we love — to have caught His mind, to breathe His spirit, to be bound up with His glory.

Beyond What You See

You may feel limitations within your flesh but you must look to that great world which lies beyond you as your scope. You will receive freedom because your faith is going out above the smallness's which surrounded you, to receive the satisfying things to come. It will not be difficult to carry out these principles. You must apply them to the right performance of any of the obligations of life. It needs no words to show that whatever is done in this freedom will not only be done better, but it takes from that freedom a character which comforts well with a member of the family of God; and which at once makes it edifying to Him, and acceptable and honoring to your heavenly Father.

Reflections For Your Journey

- Define what freedom means to you.

- Identify what you want from life.

- Identify what's keeping you from living the life you desire.

- Get the necessary steps to achieve your goal.

- Don't wait on anyone to do it for you.

- Celebrate your accomplishments.

- Develop a plan for your life to remind you what you want.

Beyond What You See

Journal

Lynn Barnes

Chapter Eleven
Pregnant & Afraid

"Every burden is a blessing."
~Walt Kelly

Things got better for me. I started high school and to top it off, I had family that was there with me. I went to school with Gina my best friend in the whole wide world. We became friends from a fight that I had in the seventh grade. It was on one of my many moves from Cali to St. Louis. I wasn't in school long, but it was long enough to where we remembered each other.

Whenever I did attend school, we would either be in the same school, class or same neighborhood.

One day I felt sick and weak, plus I was tired all the time. My appetite picked up though. I slept in my Spanish class every day. It was the weirdest thing, because I would be fine in my first period class, but as soon as I got to my second period Spanish class, I couldn't stay awake. Like clockwork, I would wake up at the end of class.

A classmate who sat right next to me said, "Sleeping again huh, you sure you're not pregnant?"

"Shut up!"

"No I'm not."

"Mmm mm," he said with a smirk.

The thought of being pregnant haunted me, but if I was, I knew it was Matthew's baby. I was terrified. I called my mom who had moved back to California.

"Hey mom!"

"Hey baby, how are you?" mom asked.

"I'm okay I guess, I've been sick. I miss you," I replied.

"I miss you too, what's wrong?"

"Are you pregnant?"

"How did you…"

"A mother's intuition," mom said.

"I felt it, and I can hear it in your voice."

"Oh, you can hear it in my voice that I'm pregnant?" I asked.

"No, Lynnie, I can hear something's wrong in your voice."

"I'm on my way," mom insisted.

"Well, I don't even know if I'm pregnant or not, I've just been feeling sick."

"I'm on my way," she responded.

My mom shocked me by flying in two days later. I don't know how she did it, but she did. For the first time in a long time I saw how much my mom loved me. That morning, I went over my Grams house. My mom was in the kitchen.

"Hi baby."

"Hi mom," I responded.

"Come here."

She put her arms around me and held me so tight.

"How do you feel?"

"I'm okay I guess."

"When do you want to tell your father?"

"Never, I mean, can we find out first?" I asked.

My mom smiled. I thought she would say, *no baby, I'll take care of it.*

But nope, instead she said, "Yes, and once we do, we need to tell him."

"It will be okay, I promise."

Not Again

That night, while watching my sister Bran, things became too familiar when Darius made his way downstairs. He tried to touch my breast and fondle me while I had my sister in my arms.

"Darius!" I screamed.

Before I could get the word, "No" out of my mouth, my mom said, "What the hell are you doing?"

I couldn't believe it. Instead of being embarrassed and mortified, I was relieved. It was out and he couldn't hide it anymore. It took me back to that darkness I suppressed so long ago. I thought I had escaped it, but it was back again. I just cried.

Darius ran upstairs to the dinning room and my mom ran after him. As I finally made my way upstairs, I walked out to the porch with tears in my eyes. My Aunt Sherrie, Kayla and my mom were already there.

"Is this true?" My aunt yelled.

"Why are you lying?" yelled Kayla.

"I'm not lying, why would I lie about that?" I replied.

Kayla ran in the house, up the stairs. I ran in after her and saw Darius standing still in a daze in the dining room.

"Lynnie I'm sorry."

"Darius, how could you do me like this, I'm your cousin, and I… I might be pregnant by Matthew."

"What are you going to do?" Darius asked.

"I don't know Darius. All I know is I'm scared."

"Lynnie, I'm so sorry. I know you may hate me, but I'm so sorry."

He left out the house and before I could move, I heard the slow taps of footsteps coming down the stairs. It was Kayla with tears running down her face.

"I can't believe you were telling the truth."

"Why would I lie about that?"

"I know. I'm sorry I didn't believe you," Kayla said.

"It's okay, I wouldn't have believed me either, I mean that's your brother."

She gave me hug and I hugged her back.

"You're pregnant?" Kayla asked.

"I don't know. Momma's taking me to find out tomorrow."

I Can't Be Pregnant

While sitting in the doctor's office, my heart was heavy. I didn't want to be pregnant. How could I let this happen? I was terrified. God please don't let me be pregnant. The nurse came in to take my blood.

"It won't take long for the result okay, so hold tight and I'll be right back."

It seemed like eternity before the doctor came in.

I was hoping the nurse would come back in and say, "Well, you're not pregnant… false alarm," or something to that nature, but nope the doctor came in with that clipboard and said, "CONGRATULATIONS!"

I must have zoned out because I saw his lips moving but I could no longer hear words coming from them. It was time to tell my dad. I didn't want to face him. I had already begged to live with him, and now I could be going back to live with my mom. We told my dad together, well mom did all the talking.

The only thing I remember him saying was, "Well, she's getting an abortion."

Then he took me to Planned Parenthood on Grand Ave.

The Effects of Being Me

I couldn't believe this was happening. Once again, I was violated. My control and sense of security had been taken away by Darius. I stopped caring at that moment. What did I have to change or fix about myself? How would I be acceptable and avoid this from happening? How could I get my control back?

I didn't know who I could trust. I felt so alone, like no one cared. I must have been less than nothing if I had no one to love me. I didn't know what to do. I felt unwanted and my feelings of self-worth were diminishing fast and I was becoming empty inside. I felt like everything had been taken from me and I was losing. I was tired of crying and the thoughts that repeated in my mind were filling me with anger and bitterness. I was so lost that I wanted to kill myself. I was irrelevant and invisible, so who would even care?

Since I was a young girl, I was always searching my mother's face for clues to who I was, but I didn't like what I saw. As I got older I continued to search for my reflection in her eyes. I never knew how difficult it would be to alter self-concepts created from childhood, but I knew it was necessary. It's difficult when we rely on others' impressions to nurture our views about ourselves, especially when those impressions are negative ones.

I was mortified about what my cousin had done to me. Now that my mother caught him and everyone knew, I was embarrassed and relived all at once. I didn't want Kayla to hate me. I felt like my secret was hurting my family. Something had to be wrong with me. I had a lot of anxiety. It made me and everyone else in my family uncomfortable to face the truth.

I felt like I let my father down. I was so scared to tell him about the pregnancy because I knew he would judge me and I was just beginning to build a relationship with him. The only option I had was to abort the baby. I didn't have time to process what was happening, which may have contributed to being able to end several more pregnancies later.

The one thing that made me feel good through this entire situation was realizing my mom still had a mother's intuition. Even though she had not been much of a mother to us, our real mom was buried deep inside. That allowed me to see her a little differently. I felt loved when she dropped whatever she was doing to come to my rescue. It was the feeling I had yearned for. It was the thing that was missing in my life. I hated that I had to be pregnant to get it, but I appreciated it. For the first time in a long time, I saw how much my mom loved me.

The physical, mental and spiritual effects following sexual abuse was difficult to cope with. I felt shaken like I was not in my body. My trust was breached and my developing brain was traumatized.

Letter to My Younger Self

Lynnie,

Although you feel like nothing good is happening, you are still growing and developing into who God needs you to be. Don't become consumed with why this happened to you, but instead say, "Why not me?" You have nothing to be ashamed of — the molestation was not your fault under any circumstances. Remind yourself how strong you are. You have handled responsibilities and situations that would break most people down and make them stop, but not you. You are resilient and you have the power to change your situation. It won't happen overnight, but keep believing it will happen.

Be relieved that momma caught Darius and now you no longer have to carry that secret as a burden. You did what you could do, but know bad things sometimes happen to good people, so don't stop letting your light shine. You didn't let daddy down, the situation hurt him and he's dealing. Many people who go through traumatic events find it takes time to re-adjust and cope for a period after the event. The residual mental, physical and spiritual effects of molestation may permeate your daily life as a survivor, which make it difficult to heal. For some, there are severe effects in the immediate aftermath of an assault that may or may not last. For others, the effects of molestation come in waves and are not felt until the shock of the event wears off.

With time spent healing, developing strong positive coping mechanisms and taking care of oneself, such reactions become less severe. The short circuit stays with us long after the violence ends, and can live on in the mind, body and spirit in a variety of ways.

Coping with these effects can be overwhelming. Don't look to someone else or a substance to help you forget, but instead ask God to take your pain and give you strength to cope with the overwhelming feelings. There is no immediate relief, so don't look for it. By facing the issue and knowing it will take time to get through, you will make it fine.

It's normal to experience an array of feelings that may confuse and create more anxiety, such as anger, distrust and feeling unsafe, but through prayer give it to God and He will protect you. There's no correct way to react to these experiences. The important thing is to be patient, know this is not your fault and you are not alone. You are wanted.

Sincerely,

Lynn

Your Future Self

Freed Slave Commentary

Romans 12:2 ESV: Do not conform to the pattern of this world, but be transformed by the renewing of your mind. Then you will be able to test and approve what God's will is—his good, pleasing and perfect will.

Don't be conformed, but be transformed. The Christian is not to copy others, but to be transformed to elevate to a higher mode of existence under God's will, that He has chosen. To be *conformed to this world,* is to act as other men do, heathen who know not God; in opposition to this the Apostle urges his readers to undergo that total change which will bring those more into accordance with the will of God.

When filled with evil, lies and deceit the mind becomes evil; when informed by the Spirit, it becomes an instrument of good. It performs the process of choosing between good and evil, and supplies the information to your conscious mind. The renewed mind is acting under the influence of the Holy Spirit. The process is to first decide what the will of God is for you and your life next, choosing to act upon it. The *will of God* is the right course of action. It is good, acceptable, and perfect.

Reflections For Your Journey

✦ Trust yourself again.

✦ Acknowledge that you have been hurt.

✦ Be angry about the injustice, but don't hold on to it.

✦ Mourn what a carefree childhood might have looked like.

✦ Realize that there was nothing wrong with you.

✦ Find support.

✦ Regain control to be empowered over the one who has exerted power over you.

Beyond What You See

Journal

Lynn Barnes

Chapter Twelve
An Unwanted Trend

"There is only one happiness in this life, to love and be loved."
~George Sands

Shame surrounded me. I was engulfed by it. When my mom and dad took me to get the abortion I could tell, my shame engulfed them too. My mom wanted to shield me from judgment, but she couldn't.

As I laid on the exam table with the thin paper underneath me, I remember looking up at the ceiling and seeing pretty butterflies and, colorful birds painted on it.

"Okay, you will feel two pinches on the inside, that's to numb you up, and then you will hear a machine come on."

"Don't be scared, just take deep breaths."

"You will then feel pressure," the nurse explained.

I didn't say a word; I just kept looking at the butterflies and the beautiful birds.

The nurse that was holding my hand asked me several times, "Are you okay?"

I ignored her. It seemed like hours had passed. I looked into the light pointed down on me and I had a flash back to one of my happiest moments, my mom and I singing, "Ease on down the road" from the movie The Wiz.

Don't you carry nothing that might be a load, come on, ease on down, ease on down, down the road...

That song took me to a happy place inside my mind to help me cope.

Once it was over, I didn't feel sick anymore, not from the pregnancy anyway. I felt a sadness come over me that I could not explain. I wanted to disappear. The ride over to my grams was quiet.

"Are you hungry?" my mom asked with concern.

"Yes," I said.

"What do you want to eat?"

"I don't care."

"You want some Sara Lou's?"

"Yes," I replied.

Sara Lou's on St. Louis Avenue had the best shrimp. We got the food and continued on to my Grams house. When we walked in, I bypassed everyone and made my way upstairs. I laid down in my Grams bed and ate my food.

The nurse told me I would experience heavy bleeding for a few days and was ordered to get plenty of bed rest. It was the price I paid for what could have been a drastic life change. A change that would have required me to take on the responsibilities of an adult (even though I had already been raising my little sister for several years) while still a child. I imagined the procedure would be the hardest part. I thought the physical aspect would have shaken me. I thought I'd get into the room full of doctors and cry about the fetus coming out of my body and the person my unborn child could have been, but I felt removed.

It took my dad what seemed like weeks to talk to me. I knew he was not only angry, but disappointed. I never wanted to hurt him. I never meant to disappoint anyone. When he looked at me I hated it. I felt like, who are you to judge me? Where were you when I needed you? I spiraled downward fast from there. It was like this first abortion (because it wouldn't be my last) was the trigger that sent my life into a tail spin out of control.

    I saw Matthew again, but not just Matthew. I also dated the captain of the basketball team and football team. I didn't date them at the same time, but I could have if I wanted too. I didn't care. I became cocky and overly confident. I felt like I could date whoever I wanted to date, just because. The cheerleading squad didn't like me. Girls who weren't even on the squad, but were just friends with the squad, didn't like me either and I didn't care. I would not stay on the back burner any longer. My grades slipped, but they didn't have far to fall because I hadn't been committed to school for a long time at that point. I moved from school to school, so I stopped caring about grades a long time ago. Not that I was a bad student, I wasn't in school long enough to get it.

Meet Me After School

There was a girl named Ebony who was beautiful, and she was my friend. She was light-skinned, petite and popular. We always had good conversation and she seemed so interested in what I had to say. It all made sense when I found out she was relaying everything back to the cheerleading squad. Well, the thing was, Ebony had another friend, Talisha who dated the captain of the basketball team. His name was Fred Davis. There wasn't anything special about him. Only that he was the captain. Fred liked me and we dated off and on. But I didn't know he was dating Talisha. Had I known, I would have called it off. I was cocky but not catty. I didn't care about Fred, but I did care about friendships.

After getting their information from Ebony they plotted to fight me. It was the funniest thing ever. If only they knew my background. I was always ready to fight. I didn't start stuff, but I would not back down to anybody. I was reckless. It didn't matter who or how many.

I told Gina about this nonsense and Gina was like, "Come on, what's up, I got you!"

The word got out. I began hearing the whispers of a fight going down after school and people were pointing and looking at me.

Fred came up to me, "What's going on?" he asked.

"What do you mean?" I responded.

"You know what I mean. You're supposed to be fighting Talisha?"

"What do you care?"

"What, you don't want me fighting your other woman?" I replied.

"Lynn, it's not even like that with me and her, she likes me," Fred said.

I looked at him sideways, then said, "Whatever," and walked away.

That made me want to fight her because even if that was the truth, that means she was starting mess with me for nothing, or he may have been lying. I wanted it over. So, after school, Gina and I walked to the bus stop. There were more students than normal walking the same path. Then, out of the crowd, I see Talisha, Ebony and the squad. It was cold outside so I had on a big coat. It didn't take anything for me to take it off and hand it to Gina. I was ready! Talisha walked up and got in my face. I can't remember the exact words we exchanged, but you can only imagine the content. The next thing I remember, I was being picked up and carried away.

I was screaming and yelling, "Put me down!"

I saw Gina running towards me with my coat in her hands. The person who picked me up was strong and tall. He didn't loosen his grip on me until he walked me on the transit bus and sat me down. Gina got on the bus and paid the driver with her student tickets.

"Lynnie, are you okay?"

I'm thinking to myself, *did I get knocked out or something?* What was going on? It was Joseph, a distant friend meaning, it was a hi and bye relationship. We weren't close at all. So I wondered, why did he pick me up? Why didn't he let me fight? He told me that, he saw Talisha pull out a knife and at that moment it had become real. This girl would have killed me over a guy. I couldn't believe it.

He could have been the person who wanted to see a good fight. But instead he cared enough about me to carry me three blocks to the bus and not only that, he made sure I got on the bus. My life was spared. At that moment, I thought, this is not worth it. Being big and bad wasn't worth my life. Gina was going off.

"Girl, it's okay, calm down," I said.

Gina couldn't calm down and she was wondering why in the world I was so calm, but I couldn't explain why. When I got home, I called my mom back in California. I couldn't get a hold of her. So, I decided to talk to my brother. It was weird going to him since so much time had passed and it felt like there was distance between us. We were older now and I didn't know if we still had that special bond we once had. So I waited for him to come home to see. While I was waiting, I listened to some music. There was one particular song called; Sweet Memories by Theresa. I fell in love with that song for so many different reasons. I sat back and listened to the lyrics. I cried for so long. It seemed like it took Twan forever to get home.

Finally he was home and I was glad I wasn't alone anymore.

"Hey sis, what's wrong?"

"I...I...I," was all that came out as the words were stuck in transition. I was an emotional wreck. Not just because I could have been killed, but because I felt like I was missing so much at that moment. I missed our relationship. I missed that first feeling of being loved by Matthew and I missed my mom. I gathered myself together and had a fantastic conversation with my brother. We talked about what happened, but we also talked about what we had come through and where we were now. By the end of our conversation, we were both in tears.

The next day at school, the principal called Talisha and I into the office. I wondered why because we did nothing at school. We were quite a ways from school property. It didn't matter. The principal heard what happened with Talisha pulling out a knife and suspended her. I was just glad I didn't get suspended. My dad would have flipped out, and that's one thing I didn't want to do…hear my dad's mouth.

When my dad was angry, he had a direct tone that wasn't pleasant. My legs would shake from being scared, so not being suspended was such a relief. Over the next couple of months, I made new friends and maintained old ones. Believe it or not I forgave Talisha, Ebony and the rest of the squad. My demeanor changed, but not my confidence. I had no fear but I wasn't reckless.

No More Drama?

My freshman year came to a close, and it was the first year, in a long time I stayed in school for the entire school year. It was a wonderful experience. Yes, even though I had some bad and terrible moments. It gave me something I hadn't had in a long time…roots. I made real lasting memories.

My grades were okay. I passed and was moving on to my sophomore year. I wanted to get focused next year since I was staying and all. I promised myself that next year would be different, no drama, no boys, and no mess. The summer came, and it was a hot mess. I was still seeing Matthew, and I found out he was seeing other people.

One night, I was listening to the radio and Magic 105 had the quiet storm on; a collection of smooth and relaxing songs. Back then you could dedicate songs to your boo. So I called and dedicated Sweet Memories by Theresa to Matthew.

I must have called a thousand times until I heard the words, "Magic, what song do you want to dedicate and who do you want to dedicate it to?"

"Yes, I would like to dedicate Sweet Memories by Theresa to my boo Matthew Johnson," I responded.

Then, I sat and waited to hear my voice on the radio and the song to follow. It came on and no sooner than the song played, my phone rang.

"Why did you do that?" Matthew said with an irritated tone.

I responded, "Why?"

"Are you seeing someone else?"

"Yes, you," Matthew replied.

It didn't take me long to get it... I was the other woman, I wasn't surprised, but it hurt all the same.

"What do you mean, yes me?" I said. Although I knew what he was saying, I wanted to hear him say it.

"You shouldn't have done that!"

And that was it. He hung up the phone. I didn't hear from him for the next two months.

Still A Hot Mess

I started seeing Wheaty, a friend of Kayla's new boyfriend Gip. I wasn't over Matthew but this made it easy to bare not being with him. I've often heard it said, *In order to get over an old love, get a new love,* so I dated Wheaty. His name was Wilson, but back then, calling someone by their nickname and not knowing their real name was the norm. I enjoyed hanging out with Wheaty. It took my mind off of the drama with Matthew until he had a conversation with Matthew about me.

Why in the world would Matthew talk to my new boyfriend? I thought. Well, the word was... Matthew wanted me back and was telling Wheaty crazy stories about me, some true and some so far off I wanted to scream.

"Matthew, why would you do that?" I asked him.

"Lynnette, you belong to me. I can't see me being without you," he responded.

Was this a joke? There was a lot of nonsense and buffoonery going on. I couldn't believe this fool.

"Matthew, you need to leave me and my boyfriend alone."

"I can't," Matthew said before walking away.

I didn't know if I should have been worried. This was craziness. This guy cheated on me several times and now he is trying to come in between me and Wheaty. I was so torn, because even though, this was some freaky stalker movie situation, I still loved Matthew. He was my first everything. But how could I trust him? I didn't want to keep going back and forth, but I didn't know how to stop. Wheaty and I kept dating until I found out he was seeing his ex-girlfriend.

Why! Why does this keep happening to me? I thought. I didn't understand what I was doing wrong. Was I too loving? Was I too soft? Was I too nice? What was wrong with me? Why was it okay for guys to have sex with me, but not be in a relationship with me? I wanted to give up on everything. No more boys! I was done! That lasted all of two days.

Matthew was calling me and coming to my grandmother's house a lot. I tried not to give in, but I missed him. So, we saw each other again, but I kept my guards up.

The Hardest Summer

That summer was hard. So many bad things happened. One night, I was over my grandmother's house and Kayla and I had just gotten back from being out. Our friend Nicole came to the door. She had been crying.

"Gip is dead!"

"What!" Kayla replied frantically.

I chimed in, "No, we saw him earlier, he can't be dead."

I think it hurt me the most because the day before, we we're all sitting around on the porch. Kayla noticed a zit on

Gip's chin that had burst and we were laughing at him. He was coming down the stairs when out of the blue he hit me real hard on the leg.

"Gip, stop playing, I hate you!" I yelled.

That was the last thing I said to him. I think I cried more than Kayla. I never had a friend die. It was hard, and I felt bad for my cousin. At the funeral, we found out that Gip had other girlfriends, or maybe they liked him. I always saw him with Kayla. So, I couldn't believe it, but I wouldn't be surprised. I tried to console Wheaty, but he didn't want to be bothered. I guess his girlfriend had it covered.

It didn't take Kayla long before she started dating again and Mike was back in the picture. So that meant Matthew was around more. That didn't last long because she soon had her eye on Marlon's brother Alan. He was a cutie, but I was shocked. His brother... really?

We hung out at Nicole's house a lot. We would sit on the porch all night laughing and joking. Nicole's mom reminded me of the mom from the television show, "What's Happening." Similar to what I wish my mom had been. I loved being over there. I would say to myself, we're so lucky, we have everything we need right here. We had the grocery store, china man, Fairground Park and a liquor store all in walking distance. It couldn't get better than this. Then my mom came back.

I was excited to have my mom back. I needed her. I was a teenage girl with so many mixed emotions and feelings of confusion. My hormones were so out of whack.

She moved back in with my grandmother and at first, everything seem to come to together. She was still getting high, but the way I saw it, it was better to have a piece of a mother than no mother at all, or so, I thought.

Lynn Barnes

Effects of Being Me

My abortion was more uncomfortable and embarrassing than it was painful. I realized that I wasn't ok as I laid on the table and had flashbacks to good times. I hadn't had many good times since that moment. I had been carrying a load I needed to release a long time ago, so my progress was labored.

I felt guilty for ending a life before it had a chance. I didn't understand how I was "supposed" to feel. It was like I was trying on the life experiences of other girls and women, but none of them fit. No other person's experience could speak for my own.

My father looking at me made matters even worse. All I had wanted was my father to want me and now he looked at me like he hated me. I didn't know if he hated me, but knowing he thought I was just like my mother crushed my spirit. I never wanted to be like her. Now it felt like I was on a similar path listening to him.

My out of control spiral was fueled by desire to be noticed, accepted and loved. I felt like my cocky confidence was my guard. It allowed people not to get to close but also kept them from thinking they could hurt me.

I felt that no one was genuine; I didn't know who to trust. I never saw myself as a fighter, now I have to fight to protect myself and it's all over a boy. Maybe this is why my mom stayed with Donald. Maybe you have to fight for these boy's affection.

Almost getting stabbed was my wake-up call. It was also my opportunity to reconnect with Twan and that felt great because he had been my friend and confidant since we were small. We had sweet memories in the midst of our turmoil, which always made everything ok and it made me feel secure. It felt great to stay at a school for the entire year and establish roots. I felt like I belonged for a change.

I never wanted to be the chick on the side. When I found out I was her, it made me feel like I wasn't good enough to be the main chick. I thought Matthew loved me and I was the one. To find out I was second made me feel like I was robbed again of the opportunity to be loved, respected and cherished. I thought to get over an old love, I had to get a new love.

Losing a friend like Gip added to my trauma. I had never had a friend die, and he was the first young person I knew to die by violence. The sadness that had been surrounding me now expanded, and I felt a sense of loss that was unfamiliar and paralyzing. I began to think how short life was. It also showed me the importance of always leaving the people we love with good memories and words that uplift rather than tear down.

My mother coming to my rescue was the silver lining in what had become my chaos. I knew my mother was buried somewhere inside of the shell that was an addict and my situation brought her out. I learned that it was better to have a piece of a mother than no mother at all.

Letter to My Younger Self

Lynnie,

Don't confuse dad looking at you different with him not caring or hating you. He wants the best for you and he knows he has not always been there for you. You are his responsibility and he never wanted to fail you. When you have a daughter that gets pregnant as a teenager it's easy for a father to feel like he let you down. It may feel like he hasn't handled his responsibility as a father, but he did the best he could.

Don't confuse his demeanor and decisions with a lack of love. Although some of your actions remind him of your mother, remember she wasn't always on drugs and something attracted him to her.

Don't feel you have to act out to be noticed and loved because you don't. You have to make sure it's the right people you want to notice you. Just because they aren't recognizing you the way you desire them to, doesn't mean they cannot see you. Your cocky confidence is your protection mechanism. I know you have to guard your heart, but don't guard it to where you push people away or you become someone you weren't created to be.

There are good people in the world, and you will meet them as long as you don't close yourself off from the world. The truth is, you are a fighter, not of people but you have been fighting for the life you desire to live. There is no boy worth being stabbed over, so make sure you choose and be careful who you befriend and share things with because everyone doesn't have your best interest at heart. You are beautiful inside and out. You don't have to give your body away to be loved or noticed. Your love is something special and your body is a gift so you must treat it as such.

Remember to always cherish the relationship you have with Twan. He loves you and will always have your back.

Don't be afraid to share with him so he can continue to be a part of your life. We all need someone in our corner we can trust and who will tell us the truth even if it hurts. Twan is and will always be your rock, so lean on him as needed. Continue to relish in your sweet memories because they will get you through some rough times. Sometimes we have to look at where we came from to appreciate our progress.

Also, you are no one's side chick. You deserve to be a priority in any young man's life. If they don't make you a priority, they are not good enough for you. You are a prize. Any man would be lucky to have you. Allow no one to make you feel like you don't deserve the best. It's ok to walk away from a relationship that doesn't feel healthy. Your Prince Charming is out there and he will find you, but don't spend too much time and energy with knuckleheads in the meantime.

Recognize true love for what it is. Love is not hurtful; love is not neglect, but rather its patient and kind. Love is sustained by action. It's a pattern of devotion in the things we do for each other every day. Mom coming to the rescue was an example of love. She has sent you through a lot and will send you through more, but she is your family and she loves you.

Live your life like the sky is the limit. Don't shortchange yourself and don't let your feelings of the end stop you from living the best life now. Know you can become whatever you want to be with proper guidance and direction. If you don't have that, you won't know which way to go in life. You will do just enough if you're not pushed or challenged.

Understand that mom loved drugs because they allowed her to escape her reality which was challenging, not that this was her plan for life. Like you, she grew up in normal dysfunction. The beatings, belittling, neglect and so on, but that is her story to tell not yours. You can only share your story. So be easy on her, but stern.

Sincerely,

Lynn
Your Future Self

Unwanted Trend Commentary

1 Corinthians 13:4-8New (NIV) - 4 Love is patient, love is kind. It does not envy, it does not boast, it is not proud. 5 It does not dishonor others, it is not self-seeking, it is not easily angered, it keeps no record of wrongs. 6 Love does not delight in evil but rejoices with the truth. 7 It always protects, always trusts, always hopes, always perseveres. 8 Love never fails. But where there are prophecies, they will cease; where there are tongues, they will be stilled; where there is knowledge, it will pass away.

There are things which we count precious now, but will soon be of no value to us. There are things we know or think we know, and we pride ourselves a good deal upon our knowledge; but when we shall become older we shall set no more value upon that knowledge than a child does upon his toys when he grows up to be an adult.

Each of us has spiritual gifts. It's not important whose spiritual gifts are greater and better than the others to establish some superiority. What's most important is that we need to love one another. Not only should we love each other, but we should love everyone else as well because we are all children of God. The Corinthians are wondering whose gifts are more important or considered more spiritual. Paul is trying to tell them that all of their gifts are important, and in exercising their gifts they should make sure they are doing so with love seeping through their every action.

Love is showing empathy and sincere concern for one's community, rather than being motivated by self-interest and personal gratification. The purpose is to express the connection between humans and God's love in Christ. The issues are our lack of love for one another. Christ-like love is not represented by our actions and this lack of love is the root of all of our problems.

Reflections For Your Journey

✦ Allow yourself to feel what you are feeling.

✦ Explore your feelings (Angry, Sad, Happy, Afraid, Ashamed).

✦ Build your self-esteem.

✦ Find forgiveness in your heart.

✦ Release self-doubts.

✦ Stop replaying the past in your mind.

✦ Know what real love looks like.

Lynn Barnes

Journal

Beyond What You See

Lynn Barnes

Chapter Thirteen
Up the Block & Around the Corner

"To love an addict is to run out of tears."
~Sandy Swenson

My mom had been back for only a couple of weeks before she started disappearing. My grams would sit in the kitchen drinking her Bud Light with her sister Louis who I loved, loved, loved.

Whenever I would come over or stayed for the summer, she never greeted me without saying, "Lynnie I'm so proud of you."

Followed by saying, "You are so beautiful."

If it wasn't for my Aunt Louis telling me that, I would have never heard it and would be in jail or a prostitute out on the streets somewhere. She seemed concerned about me and what I was up to. Not that my grams wasn't, it was just different.

My grams was also my rock that always had my back. Yea, she may have put us out every now and again, but she was the mother in my life.

"Lynnette, where is Ernie (her nickname for my mother)?"

"I don't know grams."

"Now, she said she would be right back, I'm tired of this s*** here."

"She can't come back here; I don't care what nobody says," my grams said that so many times, and then my Aunt Louis would chime in to calm her down.

"Now Gladys, you don't mean that."

"S***, yes I do!"

And they would go back and forth for a while, talk about something else, then laugh and that was it. Ernestine would still be missing in action.

Waiting on Mom

Kayla was now in a relationship with Alan, Marlon's brother and I would still go back and forth with Matthew. I wasn't all that crazy for him. He was more like something to do to pass the time. My feelings for him were fading, and I began looking at other men, notice I didn't say boys.

My mom had been back for a month and it didn't take her long to develop a daily routine. She would sleep all morning, get up around twelve or one that afternoon to eat, go back to sleep for a couple of hours, then wake up and leave. Then she would return around three in the morning.

My grandma had a screen security door with black bars. You needed a key to open it and mom didn't have one, so she always needed someone to open the door when she came back. Nine times out of ten she would be late, so whoever was the designated person, would end up sleeping on the couch which was right next to the door. Why we put up with this nonsense was beyond me.

Every time my grams would ask, "Where's Ernie?"

We would answer, "Up the block and around the corner."

That's where she was, up the street and around the corner at the dope house.

Kayla and I used to sneak out of my grams house to hang out in the area where my mother spent most of her time. We went there because the guys we were dating were there too. They were the ones supplying the drugs. They knew both our mothers and they knew where they were most of the time. I didn't care where she was because she didn't care about where I was. It only made sense not to care and I think it made the situation easier to deal with.

In the meantime, I was trying to figure out what I would do about school. I was a sophomore now and wanted the year to be different. I didn't care too much about dating; I wasn't trying to be popular. I just wanted to get through it.

Last year was a mess, and I felt like it couldn't get any worse, but I was wrong. The year started off lonely because the family that always had my back in the past, either went to another school or graduated. I had to lean on my best friend Gina for sanity. I tried keeping to myself and staying out of trouble. Gina and I tried out for soccer and made the team. Then we both made the pom-pom squad, now that was the best time. Everything seemed to move along. I had no problems with anyone. I felt like I was breathing with a steady heartbeat.

Lynn Barnes

Effects of Being Me

My mother being back to her old tricks was not a surprise, but I always wished things would be different. I stopped getting my hopes up because I was tired of being disappointed. She was who she was, and I had to accept that.

My Aunt Louis and her words of encouragement kept me going and made me feel good about myself. I realized the power of positive words. That positive reinforcement helped me to feel better about myself. It let me know everything about me wasn't bad. It reminded me I had value. Her words were my motivation. It made me feel like I could exceed expectations rather than get by with the least effort required. It was the affirmation I was yearning for. Without those words, I could have ended up on the streets, selling my body, hooked on drugs or just out there lost. Those simple words saved me.

I felt like my grandmother was my rock and always had my back, but that positive reinforcement wasn't enough at the time to discourage my destructive behavior. Allowing men to disrespect me was empowering because it gave me a sense of control by pushing the limits.

My life had been about limits and bondage, now I was expressing my desire to be free. I also freed myself from worrying about my mother. Knowing she was up the street and around the corner was enough. It became the normal dysfunction in my life. I fed into that by dating the drug dealers, but felt vindicated. Everyone knew my mom was an addict, and that was something I couldn't control, so it was hard, but I hid it under the cocky exterior. Being on my own was difficult, but I was isolating myself. Trouble seemed to find me and I thought I had experienced my lowest point. Sure, I had moments of clarity but they were few.

Lynn Barnes

Letter to My Younger Self

Lynnie,

Your personal responsibility increases when you receive positive reinforcement. So, seek it out and remind yourself who you are often. Don't allow mom's drug use to stop you from reaching your true potential. I know you wish things were different, and one day they will be. Today you must use what you have to make the most of the situation. Continue to accept mom and support her in her recovery.

Allow Aunt Louis' words to meditate in your mind and your heart. Know you are beautifully made in God's image and you can do whatever you believe you can do. Surround yourself with people who will uplift you.

Positive reinforcement is a key part of your development and self-esteem. There is so much good in you, so don't be scared to share it with the world.

You must know your worth. You don't have to give yourself to these men that don't respect you or your temple. You don't need a man to make you complete or to help you get over another man. Seek God's word to be empowered and learn that you are a descendant of royalty. If you see limits they will consume your life. But you have to make sure you push the boundaries in a positive way that encourages behavior that is in line with what you want from your life.

Mom will be ok as long as you give her to God in prayer. But remember that dating the people that supply her make you an accomplice to her addiction. You don't want to be entangled with individuals that make a living from the thing you feel crippled your family. Do your best to avoid the things that will bring heartache and pain to you or the people you love. If you can't love you, no one else can and you are doomed to a life filled with disappointment and false hope.

Sincerely,

Lynn

Your Future Self

Up the Block and Around the Corner Commentary

2 Corinthians 12:9 ESV - But he said to me, "My grace is sufficient for you, for my power is made perfect in weakness." Therefore, I will boast all the more gladly of my weaknesses, so that the power of Christ may rest upon me.

God is saying His grace is all you need. It seems more in harmony with our thoughts of God, that the prayer to be relieved from pain should be refused, because it was working out a higher calling you can't get without God. Christ will remove the desires that don't line up with His will for your life and He will give you the strength to overcome all temptation that can take you further away from Him.

His power is made perfect in weakness. This means fulfilled, accomplished, completed, and finished.

God brings His sufficient and powerful grace to the relationship; all we bring is weakness. All of this is grace because we can't do anything to deserve what He does for us. And He makes sure the results are perfect and complete. You never experience the grace unless you see the need for it—and even that realization comes by grace. The power of Jesus' grace is not fully seen until weakness is fully acknowledged. The moment you are overwhelmed with your absolute helplessness is the moment you are ready to receive His grace.

There is power in His word and by reading it we ourselves have access to that power that will protect us from allowing misfortune to destroy us.

God often brings good out of evil that the reproaches of our enemies help to hide pride from us. If God loves us, He will keep us from being exalted above measure; and spiritual burdens are ordered to cure spiritual pride. This thorn in the flesh is said to be a messenger of satan which he sent for evil; but God designed it and overruled it for good. Prayer is a healing ointment for every sore, a remedy for every ailment; and when we are afflicted with thorns in the flesh, we should give ourselves to prayer. If an answer is not given to the first prayer, nor to the second, we are to continue praying. Troubles are sent to teach us to pray; and are continued, to teach us to continue in prayer.

If you want to live by God's sufficient grace, you will not catch it falling from the sky. You must go to Him when you are thirsty, He will quench your thirst. When you read His Word, and are thinking about it, His grace is flowing into you. He wants to go with you every step of the way. And when a trial threatens to overwhelm you, remember His promise: *Sufficient for you is the grace of me.* The Lord is a faithful friend, sustaining you. He is all the grace you need.

Reflections For Your Journey

- ✦ Practice faith not fear.

- ✦ Know Christ.

- ✦ Spread God's grace to cause thanksgiving.

- ✦ Avoid sin and cling to righteousness.

- ✦ Accept your imperfections.

- ✦ Feel God's unconditional love.

- ✦ Give your burdens to God.

Beyond What You See

Journal

Lynn Barnes

Chapter Fourteen
Graduation

Proverbs 19:20-21 "Listen to advice and accept instruction, that you may gain wisdom in the future. Many are the plans in the mind of a man, but it is the purpose of the Lord that will stand."

I made it through freshman and sophomore year at Roosevelt High. Bad choices, life changing experiences and all. I did not feel like I had progressed, so I decided that I needed a change of pace. I tried applying to Ladue high school were my cousin Kayla attended. To attend a school outside of my designated district I had to register at the county school district office. Going to Ladue meant I would be with my cousin, but it also meant I would have to be bused there, which was a forty-five-minute bus ride. I thought it would be effortless, and all I had to do was tell them the school I wanted to attend. To my surprise, the person in the registration office handed me a form that had three slots for three choices of schools. I had to pick which was my first, second and third choice.

Sad to say I didn't get into Ladue, instead, they placed me in Parkway Central High. So again, I would become the new kid, knowing no one. I was nervous. Even though this change was by choice, I was still going to a new school. I didn't know what to expect. Would it be like California or would it be like Roosevelt?

The school year started, and I walked through those doors confident and aware. I promised myself that I would make better choices this time. I would choose my friends wisely and take my time before dating anyone. I didn't have to worry about the whispers of how I was pregnant at fifteen or almost losing my life over a guy. No, this time around, I just wanted to be me. I wanted no drama and I looked forward to graduating.

New Normal

My mom was still out of the picture and now my sister Bran was living with us. At first, I felt like; here we go again. I got to know her all over again. Brandy was once again my mini me. When you saw me you saw her. I even used to take her to school with me. I felt like I had raised her, but now I enjoyed being with her as my baby sister and not my baby. Although my dad still made me do things for her like comb her hair, give her a bath and get her ready for school, it was not the same. I knew I was helping him, rather than doing it all.

Having my father back put a smile on my face. Even though I went through things, it felt good having him in my life. My dad never had a woman in the house again, but he dated. He worked long hours, so Twan and I were home alone a lot. Daddy clarified that we come home right after school, do our homework, chores, cook dinner and don't go outside. I tried to stick to that routine, but I disobeyed and fell short of his expectations.

Twan worked at McDonald's then Domino's. It wasn't long before I joined him and worked at Dominos too. I loved working there. I felt a sense of freedom that was so unfamiliar. My life had changed, and I was growing up in a different way. It wasn't the growing up I had to do in California or when I was over my grandmother's house. I assumed it was what normal felt like. That felt weird because it was new. I could buy my own clothes. Sure my dad bought stuff for me too, but now I could get things I wanted.

I didn't have to hear my dad say, "You need the bare necessity" speech, so it helped.

I kept my hair done and could go to the movies on the weekend. I was on cloud nine. I fell head-over-hills for an all-boys group called New Edition, who was popular at the time. I was mesmerized by Ralph Tresvant and wanted to marry him. I knew in my heart that if I ever met him, he would fall in love with me right away, but soon reality would set in. I was not marriage material. I was used and abused like Ceely from *the Color Purple*.

I hung with the popular kids at school and dated the captain of the football team. He was a tad shorter than I was, but I didn't care. He was sweet and a beast on the field. It didn't last long, but we remained friends. I was doing so much better in my classes, not all A's and B's, but not F's and that's all that mattered. I went to dances and house parties. I was being a normal teenager. I had beef with one girl at school, but it didn't come to anything. I think she was scared of me. For the longest time, people thought I was a tall freshman, so no one messed with me. When my junior year ended, I focused more on working and hanging out.

Dad-isms

My dad used to talk to us a lot about responsibilities and paying bills.

"When you get your check, put half to the side," he would say often.

What he meant was give him half and we could keep the rest. We did it for a while but figured, since we were making the money, why are we giving half to you. Little did we know, He was preparing us for the world in his own way.

See my dad did everything the only way he knew how, in his own way and time. He was not the explaining type, just the talking at you type. His logic was supposed to make sense even if it didn't.

When he said, "Don't go outside when I'm gone," that meant, "I'm trying to keep you safe, it's dangerous out there".

But what we heard was "I'm trying to control your life and I don't want you to do anything fun, ever."

And when he said, "Don't let no one in this house," it meant, "I don't want no negros in my house while I'm gone."

My dad had a soft side to him even though he had a tough exterior. He meant well. One day, I had two boys over to the house, yeah, I know, I was rebellious. We were watching T.V. when I heard a car door slam. I started not to look outside because it was too early for my dad to be home, but I looked out anyway. Low and behold I see my dad getting something out of the back seat.

"Oh no, my dad. You guys gotta hide, NOW!"

I rushed them to the back closet since my dad blocked the back door and now I see why. Once my dad came through the door, I tried to act calm and nonchalant, but my dad knew something was going on.

"Hey daddy, you're home early."

"Yea, I had to run errands. Can you run down to the car, I left my hats in the trunk."

"Yes, okay daddy."

As I walked out of the door, I felt butterflies in the pit of my stomach. I walked back in with his hats. What I saw next, made me want to run back outside the door. I saw Jerry and Matthew with their hands raised coming out of the closet. Yes, their hands were raised as if they were being escorted by the poe-poe. In that moment, I would have given anything to be back in California.

I will take beatings and hunger for a hundred Alex, I thought.

My dad opened the door and said, "Don't come back to this door again!"

He closed the door and walked in front of me, SMACK! SMACK! I felt the burning sensation as my dad slapped me from right to left across my face. As the tears started rolling down my cheeks, my dad had the most disgusted look on his face. This look was worse than when I got pregnant.

"Your just like your momma," he said.

The fear of my dad left me in that moment and it was replaced with hurt. Maybe I was just like my mom. Maybe I will end up using drugs and be with a man that will beat me and cheat on me.

"Now go to your room!" my dad said with a stern tone.

I looked at him for a moment with such regret, then walked away. Later that night, my dad came into my room and asked if I wanted to go to a baseball game. Maybe he felt bad for saying I'm just like my mom, but like I said earlier, my dad had a soft side to him with a tough exterior.

Me Against the World

I struggled as my senior year in high school began. The words that my dad said stuck with me. I rebelled even worse. I would sneak out while my dad was sleeping to hang out with my cousin Geremy. Sometimes I would not come home at all.

I would call home to talk to Twan and act like I was someone else.

"Can I speak to Jaffy Melon?"

"Who is calling?" my father would ask.

"Funky Winklebean," I would respond.

I was out of control. In my heart, I was determined not to become who my mom was, but my flesh was doing the opposite. The scary part about it was, I didn't even know how my mom ended up the way she did. I didn't care anymore, I even stopped helping with Brandy. I wanted to be better, but I would never be what my dad wanted, instead becoming what he didn't.

Beyond What You See

I stayed over my grams house off and on. I would see my mom from time to time, my Uncle Shawn and even Darius. I never held a grudge against either of them, I was too busy holding one against my dad. I ended up meeting a guy named Jodi at a track meet. He was tall, light skinned and so handsome. He would be the one I would go to my first prom with, but he would also be another person who would break my heart.

Even though my life was different from before, I hadn't changed. I still allowed whoever and whatever to happen to me. I didn't know any better. If I loved myself enough then maybe, just maybe I would have found someone to love me back.

Graduation was around the corner and I was over joyed. I never thought I would see that day. I think no one saw it coming, but God and my Aunt Louis. My dad use to call me Mallory. Mallory Keaton was the underachiever from the show *Growing Pains*. That reference along with everything else told me that he didn't think I would graduate, but here I was, ordering my cap and gown.

Twan's graduation was on the same day as mine, so we went to his graduation first. Twan wasn't feeling well at all that day and took medicine for his asthma. Little did I or anyone else know, my brother was having a major asthma attack and we would almost lose him that day. My brother was unrecognizable walking across the stage. He had swollen up two sizes. He took slow steps to get to the person holding his diploma, then he paused and tilted back before he started walking again. Once the ceremony was over my dad rushed my brother to the hospital and my mom went with me to my graduation. I thanked God for keeping my brother alive. I would have died that day too if he had.

It was time and I was ready. "Lynn Edwards." the principal called.

I briskly walked to the stage and proceeded to take that walk, my life flashed before my eyes. Each step was a flashback. I saw myself at the park with my dad, mom and brother, hearing my uncle call my name, my grandpa dying, getting robbed, living in vacant houses, seeing my mom get beat and doing drugs, living in the van, getting molested by Darius, getting pregnant and having an abortion. It seemed like my steps were in slow motion. I was not only graduating from high school, I was graduating from child hood. I would no longer hold on to what was. I reached my hand out and grabbed hold to my freedom. What now?

The Effects of Being Me

I had gone through tough times at Roosevelt High. Things were getting better but I needed a change. Going to another school made sense. I wasn't afraid of change, I was afraid of the unknown. I was used to being the new kid, but I wanted to be the new kid with nothing attached to me. There was no drama and no mistakes. I wanted everything new. I expected different relationships with the same broken mentality. I didn't want to be the product of my environment but couldn't get the environment out of me. I let my dad down again by letting those boys in the house, but he tore my heart apart when he slapped me and said I was like my mom. Even though he may not have meant it, the words destroyed what was left of me. I wondered where God was in all of this. I now know I desired a relationship with everyone but Him.

He was there waiting, holding His arms out saying, "Come back to me, hear my voice again."

I didn't know how. I felt like I was not only graduating from high school, but I was graduating from the bondage of my childhood. I thought once I crossed that stage and got my diploma that everything would be wiped away and I would be grown enough to leave.

I ended up getting put out months after graduation. I wish things could have been different, I wish I had a normal childhood, but then I realized that everything that happened to me would give me the strength, knowledge and wisdom to help others. I'm not perfect by any means, but God uses everyone and every situation to bring glory to Him. We may not see it, we question it and I promise you, we may not believe it. God is waiting to save us, He's waiting to love us. I was looking for that love from someone who couldn't give me the love I deserved. That unconditional love that only my spiritual Father could give me. I held my breath for so long, just to come up for air.

God gives over flowing air even under water. I didn't realize that then.

Matthew 11:28 God says, "Come to me, all you who are weary and burdened, and I will give you rest."

I was tired of being seen as troubled, promiscuous and boy crazy. No one knew how hurt I was, how broken I had become. I was screaming from the inside out every day for seventeen years and no one bothered to pay attention enough to hear me. I was tired and once I knew how to give it to God and ask Him for rest. I did and He gave it to me.

Letter to My Younger Self

Lynnie,

You did it! You graduated. I know it feels good. You've gone through so much and it was hard. You are stronger than you think. Times will get harder now that you're out on your own and you will go through more heart ache, trials and tribulations. Keep your feet on solid ground my love.

Your life was spinning out of control because you were use to that. Even though you felt changing schools was going to give you a new beginning. No one knew you, no one could whisper about things in the past, but you had to change you. You had to see who Lynnie was and not who your mother was. Yes, your dad spoke those words, but only out of hurt and anger. The words parents speak to their children will affect them in a positive way or a negative way. Hearing your dad say that you were just like your mom was not saying you'll end up like her, but that you were already like her, so those words would have a negative effect on you for years to come.

Words are powerful. They can either build, break or even tear down. Your dad already had a hold on your heart because you loved him so much, so his words and what he thought of you mattered. You didn't know how to handle myself as a young lady. You didn't have respect for yourself, how could you? The two people that were supposed to teach you that and so much more weren't there for you. Being there physically but not mentally is worse than being gone all together. God is protecting you right now from what He sees coming. Mom and Dad loves you so much, but they couldn't give you what they didn't grow up with. They did the best they could with what they had and knew. Keep letting your light shine even in your darkest moments.

Twan had you scared there I know, but God is a healer as well as a protector. Don't keep getting caught up in what should have been or what was. The time to find out who you are starts now. Keep your head up, not down because you will miss the signs from God.

Walk in the direction and path he has set before you. Without it, you will be lost and confused. Don't lean on your own understanding, God has a plan and purpose for your life and it will take time to walk in it, but don't be scared. God will be with you every step of the way holding his arms out for you. If you stumble and fall, he will pick you up.

There will be many who will try to distract you and destroy you, but you have been there and done that. Now you know how to see people for who they are. Trust your judgement.

Sincerely,

Lynn
Your Future Self

Lynn Barnes

Graduation Commentary

Deuteronomy 31:6 Be strong and courageous. Do not be afraid or terrified because of them, for the LORD your God goes with you; he will never leave your nor forsake you.

God knows the plans for your life. So, build your kids up. Help them know who they are as children, teenagers and young adults. Don't assume that they know what's expected of them. God will guide you in doing so because like I stated earlier, kids or a gift from God.

Proverbs 22:6 Train up a child in the way he should go; Even when he is old he will not depart from it.

Reflections For Your Journey

- Make the change in you to be better.

- Speak words to encourage and not to tear down.

- Seek God and the plan he has for you.

- Know that your value is important.

- Pursue your dreams and don't have the fear of falling or failing.

- Love yourself no matter what.

- No one's perfect but God.

Lynn Barnes

Journal

Beyond What You See

Lynn Barnes

Chapter Fifteen
Celebrate Recovery

*"Some people see things as they are and say 'Why.'
I dream things that never were and say, 'Why not.'"
~George Bernard Shaw*

I became promiscuous as a teenager. I was looking for love that seemed to slip through my fingers. I repeated the unhealthy patterns I saw growing up. I recreated in adult relationships some of the feelings I knew in childhood. As children, we first come to know and understand what love means. But, the lessons we picked up may not have been straightforward. The love we knew as children may have come entwined with other, less pleasant experiences, like being controlled, feeling humiliated, being abandoned, never communicating, not having stability, and suffering from hunger.

I clung to familiar things and ideas, which caused me to miss opportunities, relationships or experiences that could have helped me grow, but instead, I felt oppressed. I had a love void in my life and I thought I filled it by giving up my body to get love. By not having a real father figure in my life I was crying out for that love and attention. The void I was missing was God and without Him I was doomed to repeat the cycle, replaying generational curses like my favorite song.

My mood often depended on my mother's mood. I walked on eggshells to ensure she was happy with us and if we did anything she didn't like, we got beat. I always needed to feel like I was needed or wanted to feel complete, valued and appreciated. What I didn't see was that who I was, was enough. I was made whole in Him and His mercy.

Misguided

We like to feel attractive, admired, and interesting to those we get intimately attached to. But, if you require the approval and compliments of someone else to validate your worth, it is safe to say you should look for a spiritual value in life. We should not require others to tell us how beautiful we are, that is a recipe for disaster.

I bounced from relationship to relationship, choosing guys that weren't right for me, but feeling like I needed to oblige them because they showed me attention. In exchange, I would get the connection I was yearning for. By doing this I was trying to fill the spiritual void by seeking new men instead of seeking spiritual growth.

I often ignored my values or bent over backward to keep someone in my life romantically. It was clear I depended too much on their role in my life. The void comprised the empty, lonely feelings that came from holes in my heart and soul. Holes from resenting my mother and the addiction that was destroying her, wounds of molestation, breakup, death, moving, lack of connection, and losing my sense of stability.

Sometimes voids can also stem from something much deeper, like a lack of connection with family growing up, a childhood trauma, or hurt caused by someone in our past. The things that guys found the most attractive about me, I accentuated. I knew they wanted to have sex with me, so I gave it. Without defining your true self, you give up control and allow others to dictate or influence your attitude and behavior. Much of what you accept is based upon what other people will define you as.

My self-confidence was stunted. I wasn't familiar with what a positive expression of love felt like, therefore I didn't develop an appreciation for my looks or my body. My sense of self was tainted and my portrait of a loving relationship was distorted and dysfunctional. I needed a glimpse of approval from somewhere because I didn't get it from daddy.

It was difficult to relate to men because I looked to find recognition from them. This thought led me down an early path of promiscuity. My actions made me feel bad, but I moved to man after man, hoping one would give me what I never had as a child…validation of myself for myself.

My painful early life experiences caused me to experience hurtful feelings toward myself. As I grew up, I adopted a pattern of destructive thoughts toward myself. I allowed those thoughts to impact my behavior and shape the direction of my life. I was preventing myself from living the life I wanted to live and becoming the person, I wanted to be.

My self-worth was based on how I saw myself. I thought so little of me.

My Worth

It took becoming an adult and hitting rock bottom in my own life before I could understand that I'm worth more than what others said or treated me like I was worth. I didn't have a route to happiness and fulfillment, but I was determined to find it. By not knowing myself I was left open to challenges that made me feel lost all over again.

I was misdirected in life and made many bad life decisions, but those bad decisions would lead me to victory. Society measured me against others and I did the same thing to myself, rather than recognize my value.

I had to remember that optimism and the ability to remain hopeful are essential to resilience and the process of recovery. I was a girl raised without a father. I suffered from low self-esteem, an unreliable sense of self and I sought attention from men. I internalized this into my own messed up patterns and made mistakes. I had to learn that, who I am is up to me; my parents are not responsible for my decisions.

It's been a very long journey and imperfect process, but I have decided to forgive my dad for not being there for me, for not giving me all I thought I deserved and my mom for not being there mentally and protecting me. I also forgave myself for carrying years of self-righteous anger and for all the things that have come up since.

Against All Odds
I was determined to not allow the absence of my father drive me to become someone I didn't want to be. I wanted to become a woman that might just choose the company of a partner who is kind, rather than one who shows superficial attention or one who loves me for who I am, rather than what I look like. I wanted to be a woman that took risks, believed in herself and walked a little taller in the world.

I heard God referred to as my Heavenly Father, but I didn't know how to tap into His power. I was lost in a sea of labels, emotions and misguided ideas of who others told me I was or should be.

I loved my mother, but knew she had a problem. How she responded to my cries influenced how I thought and how I was seen by others. As children, we behave in ways that perpetuate what we have experienced. I experienced a lot of hurt, pain and sadness, so I behaved accordingly. I felt neglected by both parents even though I lived with my mother. Drugs had a grip on her that changed her. My mother didn't respond to my needs and that destroyed my confidence, while her abusive relationship shaped my views of men and relationships which would soon have detrimental consequences.

Your emotions which are an offspring of your self-worth, determine how you feel about yourself. Your self-worth affects your potential to be the best you and live the life that He created you to live.

Power in my Abuse

Stop comparing yourself to others and evaluating your every move. The voice inside your head is called your inner voice. It tells us we are worthless or undeserving of happiness. You must challenge your inner voice and recognize when it's from God versus something you're telling yourself. That will only cause you pain, sadness and make you believe you are less than.

Self-worth is more about valuing your worth as a person. It's about who you are, not about what you do or have. When your self-worth is less, you often see the world in a poor light and develop a negative perspective. You must remember to see the good in each situation.

On this journey, I've experienced trauma that resulted from my mother's drug abuse and the sexual abuse I lived through. I've experienced a syndrome that didn't just affect me and my family, but all of our society. Molestation is such a shame-filled concept. Our culture suppresses molestation because no one wants to talk about it due to the shame associated with it.

Today, I celebrate my recovery and thank Christ for the clarity to see the purpose in my situation. I celebrate God's healing power in my life through His principles. By applying His principles, I have experienced freedom from past hurts, habits, and hang-ups creating peace, serenity, joy and a stronger personal relationship with God and others. I found a safe place to share my struggles, a place where I can take off

Beyond What You See

my masks. I found a place where the words, *Nobody walks alone*, changed my life and it can do the same for you. Use my testimony to embrace and celebrate your recovery to heal what no one else can see.

The Effects of Being Me

I was misdirected in life and lacked the feelings of worthiness, therefore made a lot of bad life decisions. Society measured me against others and in turn, I did the same thing to myself rather than paying attention to my own value. This was a process of change through which I was able to improve my mental health, wellbeing, and life overall. I am now driven to reach my full potential.

I had to have hope and believe that the challenges I faced could be overcome. My recovery was built on my strengths, talents, coping abilities, resources, and inherent values. I had to address all of me to be whole. I felt that my journey was highly personal and occurred via many pathways, but finding God was the best path.

Recovery pushed me to practice self-care by realizing I had value and could live the life I desired no matter how it began. My story wasn't over as long as I had breath in my body. I practiced continual growth and improvement to overcome setbacks. I learned that setbacks are a natural part of life and that resilience becomes a key component of recovery.

I found the strength to cope with adversity and adapt to challenges and changes. I developed the capacity not only to cope with life's obstacles, but also to be better prepared for the next stressful situation. Through all the pain I encountered, I can say I am a better person because of my circumstances. I made lemonade out of the lemons I was given and as a result, I now have a big wonderful family, moments of grace, easy love, the unexpected freedom in my heart, which is a sort of self-love. I'm breaking the cycles that have held my family back for generations. They are all crushed in the name of Jesus!

Lynn Barnes

Letter to My Younger Self

Lynnie,

You must figure out what you are good at and what sets you apart from everyone else. Remind yourself that you have a reason for being here, but it's up to you to find it. Your self-worth should also take into account the unique qualities that make you. God created you this way for a reason. You are unique like your fingerprint and your self-worth determines your self-esteem, which I view as the motivation that dictates your mood.

Treat yourself with the same kindness and compassion as you would treat a friend. If the words you hear sound like words that condemn or don't lead you to victory, dismiss that voice because it isn't of God. You must know and remember who God says you are to identify yourself.

God gave everyone gifts and talents, that means you too! Your gifts and talents are things that you love to do, come easy to you, and you are good at doing. These are things you enjoy and were created to do.

There are so many women that grew up like you did. The key word being "women". They began as little girls in similar situations, if not worse, and some got through it. But there are some that didn't get through it and now hold bitterness, resentment and feelings of low self-worth in their adult lives.

When you can't see past the superficial things that look like mountains that keep you stuck and feeling less than, focus on the fact that you are not your situation or what you're experiencing. You are bigger than your situation because your God is bigger, and only through Him will you be able to see past those things to increase your low self-esteem.

Sincerely,

Lynn

Your Future Self

Beyond What You See

Celebrate Recovery Commentary

The Eight Beatitudes of Jesus Gospel of St. Matthew 5:3-10

Jesus Christ gave us the eight Beatitudes in the Sermon on the Mount, recorded in the Gospel of Matthew, the first Book of the New Testament of the Bible. The Beatitudes of Jesus provide a way of life that promises salvation, but they also provide a path of peace in the midst of our trials and tribulations on this earth.

> Blessed are the poor in spirit, for theirs is the kingdom of heaven.

> Blessed are they who mourn, for they shall be comforted.

> Blessed are the meek, for they shall inherit the earth.

Lynn Barnes

Blessed are they who hunger and thirst for righteousness, for they shall be satisfied.

Blessed are the merciful, for they shall obtain mercy.

Blessed are the pure of heart,
for they shall see God.

Blessed are the peacemakers, for they shall be called children of God.

Blessed are they who are persecuted for the sake of righteousness, for theirs is the kingdom of heaven.

Reflections For Your Journey

+ Be kind to yourself.

+ Acknowledge your achievements.

+ Mistakes and Failures are a part of life.

+ Create a mindset to see the opportunity in your adversity.

+ Don't compare yourself to others.

+ Seek help always.

Lynn Barnes

Journal

Beyond What You See

Made in the USA
Columbia, SC
23 January 2018